DAY STARTERS
FOR MOMS

60 DEVOTIONS TO HELP YOU LOVE YOUR
KIDS AND KEEP YOUR SANITY

Edited by Shelley Hendrix

FaithHappenings Publishers

Scripture quotations marked (ESV) are from The Holy Bible, English Standard Version® (ESV®), copyright © 2001 by Crossway, a publishing ministry of Good News Publishers. Used by permission. All rights reserved.

   Scripture quotations marked (GNT) are from the Good News Translation in Today's English Version- Second Edition Copyright © 1992 by American Bible Society. Used by Permission.

   Scripture quotations marked (HCSB) are taken from the *Holman Christian Standard Bible®*, Copyright © 1999, 2000, 2002, 2003 by Holman Bible Publishers. Used by permission.

   Scripture quotations marked (NASB) are taken from the New American Standard Bible®, Copyright © 1960, 1962, 1963, 1968, 1971, 1972, 1973,1975, 1977, 1995 by The Lockman Foundation Used by permission.

   Scripture quotations marked (NIV) are taken from the Holy Bible, New International Version®, NIV®. Copyright © 1973, 1978, 1984, 2011 by Biblica, Inc.™ Used by permission of Zondervan. All rights reserved worldwide

   Scripture quotations marked (NKJV) are taken from the New King James Version®. Copyright © 1982 by Thomas Nelson. Used by permission. All rights reserved.

   Scripture quotations marked (NLT) are taken from the *Holy Bible*, New Living Translation, copyright ©1996, 2004, 2007, 2013 by Tyndale House Foundation. Used by permission of Tyndale House Publishers, Inc., All rights reserved.

   Scripture quotations marked (The Message) are taken from THE MESSAGE. Copyright © by Eugene H. Peterson 1993, 1994, 1995, 1996, 2000, 2001, 2002. Used by permission of Tyndale House Publishers, Inc.

Cover Design: ©Angela Bouma
Book Layout ©2013 BookDesignTemplates.com

Day Starters for Moms © FaithHappenings Publishers
ISBN: Softcover: 978-1-941555-07-1

This book was printed in the United States of America.
To order additional copies of this book, contact: info@faithhappenings.com

FaithHappenings Publishers,
a division of FaithHappenings.com
7061 S. University Blvd., Suite 307 | Centennial, CO 80122

Dedicated with Love to all the Moms

I never dreamed

That I could Love

Someone I hardly knew;

But that was just

Until the day

When I first laid eyes on you.

Shelley Hendrix

June 11, 1994

CONTENTS

U R a Momma So . . .

Jennifer Strickland

Y ou are a vessel to the future.

You are a molder and a shaper, a giver of gifts and grace.

You signed your name on the dotted line the day she was born.

You carried her home in fresh blankets and lace.

You became her source for snacks and juice and tissues and tears,

For whispers and sweaters and boo boos and fears.

In the dark of the night you caressed her skin, sunk into her eyes, held her close, rocked away her cries.

Yet today you wake up on the edge of 13, and there's a jagged edge seed in your heart, not seen.

It feels like all these years of giving, and there's so much more to gain.

She's scared, she's hurt, she's alone, she cries.

She questions, she wishes, she dreams, she tries.

And you keep failing though you try and you try,

Your words bounce off her; inside pieces of you die.

You want her to be ALL that she can be, to know the things she can't possibly know now.

That love is sacrifice and giving isn't free,

But even you don't know how.

So you pray until she sleeps and then pray some more.

You wish she could touch her dreams like toes kiss the shore.

Only God sees how your heart aches,

How you cannot bear for the seed of your womb to kick against you this way,

How it hurts to pour out your heart like wax, to beg change, to splinter your hands trying to build a life you can't,

How you walk away cut and bleeding when you thought you'd find grace.

It is in being a Momma that you realize, only God is farmer best,

You can till, Momma, you can break ground, you can run your hoe today,

But up to Him is the rest. You plod, you set your seed, you water, you feed.

But her heart's soil, her life's dirt, will someday be her own.

The sun will set and she will walk away like she is grown.

Only for you will she still be a babe, who upward you lift;

And you will know as you always have she is evermore a gift.

Not yours to make, not yours to take, just Momma's ground to till and rake.

Season by season, year by year, you are Momma, steward dear.

Keep planting, Momma, keep watering still,

Keep trusting that He made her by His will.

Her life is in His hands. Keep it there; He holds her near.

You can love like a river that never runs out,

You may scream, you may cry, you may beg, you may shout,

But you are picked, you are chosen, you are able, you are willing.

With your eyes fixed on Jesus, keep on mowing and tilling.

Never give up on the field of her heart.

Kneel low, plant seed, stretch tall.

Knowing who she is now is only a part

Of who she shall be;

It is not the All in All.

One day, she will see God, walk free.

As long as you love, as long as you live,

You are Momma, with grace to give.

Door always open, heart never shut,

You are His vessel, no matter what.

So if today it's sippie cups and pacifiers

Or teen hormones like raging fires,

Believe in your heart you are the farmer's best hand,

To mow this field, pull that weed, take care of this land . . .

That is your child's soul.

It is worth the sweat, the thorns, the whack of the hoe,

For some day those seeds of peace, that planting love,

Will bear fruit by way of God above.

U R a Momma, So.

TWO

Stay

Jill McSheehy

Jesus said, "Because you have seen Me, you have believed.
Those who believe without seeing are blessed."

John 20:29 (HCSB)

My husband and I sat across the table at a steakhouse from one of my best friends and her husband. She was barely able to make it through the meal due to morning sickness. I was barely able to make it through the meal due to despair. My heart ached for what she had growing inside of her. Although my husband and I hadn't been trying for a baby for all that long, it seemed like forever. My greatest fear was that my mom's seven-year struggle to conceive would be my journey as well.

I tried to be happy for my friend but my heart felt empty. Why had God visited her and given her the desire of her heart but not me? Why was I having to wait with no promise that He would even visit me?

4

"But ... Thomas (called 'Twin') was not with [the disciples] when Jesus came ... After eight days His disciples were indoors again, and Thomas was with them." (John 20:24, 26)

Thomas, for an unknown reason, was not with the disciples when Jesus had first appeared to them after he was raised from the dead. When the disciples tried to tell Thomas that they saw Jesus, he could not believe. I feel for Thomas. Jesus visited the others. He was the only one left out. For eight days—eight days!—Thomas had to live with the fact that the others had seen Jesus but he hadn't. Why didn't Jesus at least appear to him like he did to Mary Magdalene?

What a lonely, heart-wrenching eight days. Was he not as special as the others? Had Jesus forgotten about him? I'm sure his thoughts were all over the place with despair. But he stayed. Eight days later, Thomas was with the disciples. He didn't flee or run away. Even though he must have felt like the black sheep, he stayed.

"Even though the doors were locked, Jesus came and stood among them. He said, 'Peace to you.' Then He said to Thomas, Put your finger here and observe My hands. Reach out your hand and put it into my side. Don't be an unbeliever, but a believer.' Thomas responded to Him,'My Lord and my God!'" (John 20:26b-28)

Finally, after eight long days, Jesus appeared to Thomas. And when He did, his lesson to Thomas was on belief. Thomas could understand the darkness of unbelief, the wanting to believe but the inability to do so. I have to believe that in Thomas's subsequent ministry, he used that eight-day experience as He shared Jesus with others. Historical evidence shows that Thomas traveled to India to preach the gospel. As he shared Jesus with others, He had an ability to understand the unbelief that would come from a people who had never seen Jesus. But he could point to Jesus' next statement:

"Jesus said, Because you have seen Me, you have believed. Those who believe without seeing are blessed," (John 20:29).

The reason Thomas saw Jesus the second time He appeared to His disciples was that he stayed. In those agonizing months of waiting for God to visit me with a child, I poured my heart into studying women of the Bible who were barren. Although I was not barren, it helped me to stay in the Word and to press into Jesus as I waited. I didn't run away in despair or resentment. And when the time came, God visited me. My husband and I found out we would have our first child.

When you see Jesus' presence with others, when you feel forgotten, when you can't believe even though you want to—STAY. Just as Jesus had a purpose in Thomas' eight days, he also has a purpose in your wait. He'll come at the right time. He may not always answer your prayer exactly how you expect, but He will come. He hasn't forgotten.

Prayer

Dearest God, thank you for your promise that you are always with me. Thank you for being faithful even when my faith fails. As I serve you as a mother to the ones you've entrusted to my care and nurture, help me to do so out of the overflow of the love I receive from you so that in seasons of waiting—and not seeing—I can still declare, 'I believe.' In Jesus' Name, Amen.

THREE

I Forgot to Get Dressed Today

Katie Gibson

Above all, clothe yourselves with love, which binds us all together in perfect harmony.

Colossians 3:14 (NLT)

Have you ever forgotten to get dressed in the morning?

I have. Yep. This morning I forgot to get dressed.

I realized it as I was loading my kids into the car to take my "Middle Little" to school.

"Hurry up!" "Get in the car!" "Hurry!" "Are you listening to me??" "5 . . . 4 . . . 3 . . . 2 . . ."

After nearly five minutes of wrangling them into the car, IT happened: "Mom, I'm still hungry. I need a granola bar."

Foot on the brake, ready to back out, I flipped.

That was when it hit me—I forgot to put on my patience this morning.

(Phew. I bet you're relieved, right?)

Saying I forgot to put on my patience doesn't seem nearly as severe as forgetting to put actual clothes on my body, right? But if you dig into God's Word, you'll find that getting spiritually dressed is nothing to scoff at.

In Colossians 3:12 Paul says, "Since God chose you to be the holy people he loves, you must clothe yourselves with tenderhearted mercy, kindness, humility, gentleness, and patience." Then, in verse 14 he emphasizes, "**Above all, clothe yourselves with love, which binds us all together in perfect harmony.**"

Tenderhearted mercy (compassion), Kindness, Humility (putting others first), Gentleness (moderate—not excessive or intense), Patience—we are to wear these.

And just like physical clothing, we are supposed to wear them every day—without fail.

Why? Because like boots on a rainy day or a tank-top in the summer, we have to be prepared for what life may throw at us. We would be completely uncomfortable if we went outside in 23-degree weather without coats, right?!

Let's not miss what Paul said first: "Since God chose you . . ."

He chose YOU. You are His, and you represent Him to the rest of the world.

That's a high honor and a pretty intense calling, right? One that requires preparation. Intention. Clothing.

Had I put on my love and patience this morning, my response to my son probably would have been more gracious and loving—more like the Father I want him to see through me. And we would have avoided unnecessary shame, frustration, and tears.

I don't always get it right, but I think that if I were diligent to get dressed spiritually every morning, I would probably get it right more often. Not in my own power—but in the love, mercy, kindness, humility, patience, and gentleness He openly provides every day.

What about you—did you know there is an entire closet at your disposal every morning, filled with everything you need to face the day?

Don't make the same mistake as me and walk around spiritually bare! Let's run to the closet, desperate and dependent on God's provision, as we seek to live out lives that honor Him.

"Since God chose you to be the holy people he loves, you must clothe yourselves with tenderhearted mercy, kindness, humility, gentleness, and patience. Make allowance for other's faults and forgive anyone who offends you. Remember, the Lord forgave you, so you must forgive others. Above all, clothe yourselves with love, which binds us together in perfect harmony." Colossians 3:12-13

Prayer

Lord, forgive me for so often neglecting to put on the love, compassion, kindness, humility, gentleness, and patience you have given so freely. I want to honor you in the way I live my life before my family, my friends, and the people I will encounter today. Help me to walk in your strength, your love, your provision today. In Your Name, Amen.

FOUR

Teaching Our Little Ones (and Ourselves) About Forgiveness

Shelley Hendrix

'Come now, let us reason together," says the LORD: 'though your sins are like scarlet, they shall be as white as snow; though they are red like crimson, they shall become like wool."

Isaiah 1:18 (ESV)

When my firstborn was only two years old and some change, she became a big sister. All of a sudden, the nearly undivided attention she was accustomed to had to be shared with a new person in our lives. Most of the time, this was okay with her . . . until bedtime. That little, mostly angelic creature would approach me while I was nursing her little sister with the demand to "put that baby down and hold ME!"

We began to get a bit of a routine down and a few months in, I was feeling pretty good about my mothering skills because I had gotten the girls dressed and ready to go; one playing nicely while the other got in a late nap so we could attend a special event together at church. My husband was going to come home quickly to freshen up so we could all get out the door in time to be on time—a luxury for a new mom with a young family.

When I was nearly finished getting myself ready, my two-and-a-half-year-old came to me with what I initially assumed was diaper contents all over her. Greenish-brown yuck ALL. OVER. HER.

That would have been bad enough if that had been what it was— it would have been unpleasant to deal with, but fairly simple to clean up and take care of before Daddy got home and we needed to be ready to jet out the door.

But it wasn't poo.

It was paint.

Oil paint.

And she wasn't coming to see me with remorse for getting into her father's oil paints. No, she was coming to me with pride to show me her artful masterpiece downstairs.

This child painted walls, carpet, doors, doorframes, and probably the cat!

This presented me with a huge dilemma:

How do I, as a mom, let her know this was absolutely NOT okay, while also not shaming her in the process?

How do I let her know this is a big deal without making it too big of a deal?

She was a smart girl, but she was only two and a half!

I honestly don't remember exactly what happened. I do know I was upset, frustrated, and remorseful that I had not kept her closer to me while I was getting ready. I didn't lose my cool and yet I was stern with her to let her know that she couldn't, under any circumstances, play with her Dad's paints. She's always had a tender heart and this little girl got the message loud and clear. While I appreciated her desire to be creative, it was not going to be acceptable to go all Rembrandt all over our home.

She tearfully apologized. I hugged her.

This wasn't the end of the world. It was an inconvenience, but it wasn't such a big deal.

The evidence of her 'creativity' remained until we could tend to it all properly. (We eventually got rid of the carpet with her handprint because there was just no way to get it out.)

I moved on and didn't think much about it.

A couple of weeks later, we were riding down the road, and she had been pretty quiet (which even now, at almost twenty-one years of age, is still uncommon. And, yes, I know she comes by it honestly). Some time went by and her little voice, partly quivering, said, "Mommy, I'm so sorry I got into Daddy's paints."

I was so surprised. I had no idea she had even been thinking about it. She had apologized a few times after it all happened, but I had explained to her that I forgave her and it was all going to be okay. I knew she was really sorry for it and that I loved her just as much after as I loved her before the whole thing happened.

I said, "Amelia, honey, I forgave you for that." I could tell this incident was haunting her. Shame had crept in with its ugly accusations and my little one was not equipped to combat it on her own.

I asked, "Do you know what forgiveness means?"

"No."

"It means that I know what you did, and yes it was wrong; but it also means that I'm not going to bring it up again. You are still my

Amelia and I'm still glad you're mine. You don't have to be afraid, sweet girl."

How much like a two-year-old are we at times? Our shame whispers to us that we've never been sorry enough for things we have done . . . or that bad things happened to us as punishment for _____ . . . or that we should be afraid because eventually the other shoe is going to drop.

Just like I wanted my daughter to understand my forgiveness meant she didn't have to fear that I was going to allow this to come between us, God wants us to know that because we stand forgiven already, nothing we've ever done nor will ever do can stand between us and Him. He loves us! He accepts us just as we are. Our need to repent is not to get Him to want us around again, our repentance is for US because we can't experience His love for us in relationship while we're stubbornly holding onto pride.

Prayer

Dear Forgiving Father, how we often forget how good you truly are. Give us the courage to trust that we stand fully forgiven with you and give us the strength to offer genuine, heartfelt forgiveness towards those who have offended us. In Jesus' Name, Amen.

FIVE

Sometimes Parenting Feels Like a Lot of Wrong Turns

Gillian Marchenko

*Let all bitterness and wrath and anger and clamor and slander be put away
from you, along with all malice. Be kind to one another, tenderhearted,
forgiving one another, as God in Christ forgave you.*

Ephesians 4:31-32 (ESV)

My ten-year-old daughter, Zoya, participated in the school band her fifth grade year. She chose to play the trumpet, which thrilled me, having been a trumpeter myself in my youth. I located my instrument from high school and cleaned it up for her use.

The class started. She learned how to read music. Before long we heard amazing hits such as "Three Blind Mice" nightly. It was either that or a fog horn? Either way, I couldn't wait for her first band concert. The day arrived, and I was depressed because I am a mother who fights depression and, well, that just happens sometimes. But I wanted to be there for my daughter, so I took a shower, put on jeans and a

14

shirt, and situated myself in the driver's seat to go to the concert. We had more than enough time and simple directions. Just two turns. Fool proof. So off we went.

Zoya, her trumpet, and me singing along to the radio while I secretly swabbed my sweaty face with balled up Kleenex. Twenty minutes later we were still driving. I got nervous. We had to have been close to our destination. Or did we miss it? It wasn't supposed to be this far away. We drove deeper into the south side of Chicago and I started to shake.

"Mom, are we almost there? We're going to be late." Zoya sat shotgun. Her face moved from mild amusement towards a worried expression. "Let me call Papa and ask him," I tried to say nonchalantly. I'm sure my voice came out shrill and pinched. My husband broke the news when I called. "Gillie, the concert is the other way, across town. You should have turned right. You turned left."

I looked at the clock on the dash. Warm-ups for Zoya's band were to start any minute at the concert. We were at least thirty minutes away. We were going to miss it.

"Zoya, I turned the wrong way," I whispered as I pulled the car over to change directions. "I'll drive as fast as I can. Maybe you'll make it for the actual show." My daughter started to cry. I apologized profusely. The trumpet sat in the backseat. An inanimate object that was going to stay inanimate. I couldn't believe my mistake. I wanted to be inanimate too.

We drove and watched the minutes tick by. By now the band would be playing "Are you sleeping, Brother John?" and other songs. We definitely were missing Zoya's first band concert. I joined in on the crying.

Wrong Turns

Just like I made a wrong turn for Zoya's band concert, I make a lot of wrong turns when it comes to parenting my kids. Oh, I want to do well. But I'm human. I overreact and underreact. I get frustrated. I get sick. We all screw up. We sin. We struggle.

As a mom, I need to understand and accept that I will make mistakes. But I also am learning that I shouldn't hide my failures and struggles because they are a huge part of life. And if handled correctly, they are a great way to teach our girls that although life doesn't always go according to plan, it is still worth living for the glory of God. If we are willing to show our kids all of us, the good, the bad, and the ugly, then they can get a better understanding of grace.

So, what happened with Zoya's band concert? We missed it. We missed it by a long shot. I looked over at my sweet girl as we zoomed across town. She was staring out the window and wiping tears from her cheeks. "Zoya, I'm sorry. I really screwed up. And I am disappointed too. I couldn't wait to see you play your trumpet on stage. Tell you what . . . It's not a band concert, but how about we catch a movie?" Zoya's face brightened as I turned into the parking lot of our neighborhood theater.

That night she got popcorn *and* pop *and* candy. Was it great parenting? Who knows? And really, who cares? We hung out in the arcade afterward. I gave her quarters and watched her feed the machines. We giggled as the Pac-Man ate the dots. We high-fived when she got high score on another game. I hugged her and tried to remember the moment and the day, even though it was painful and embarrassing. Because I think I would rather remember then forget. And I know a lot more wrong turns are in our future. That's just life.

The other day Zoya and I drove by the theater. "Hey Mom, remember when we missed my first band concert and went to a movie?" she asked. "Yeah, I remember," I replied while pulling the car up to a stop sign. "Even though we took a wrong turn, it ended up being a pretty great day."

Prayer

Dear Heavenly Father, thank you that you are aware of our humanity, our frailty and our inability to get it right at every turn. Thank you for allowing U-turns and for offering redemption when we miss the mark. In Jesus' Name, Amen.

SIX

Faith, Trust, and Pixie Dust

Jessica Wolstenholm

Let your light so shine before men, that they may see your good works and glorify your Father in heaven.

Matthew 5:16 (NKJV)

'All the world is made of faith, and trust, and pixie dust."

J.M. Barrie, Peter Pan

My kiddos are so into Peter Pan and Jake and the Neverland Pirates right now. We watch the show all.day.long and the movie, sometimes, multiple times in one day. It's no wonder, then, that I've had the idea of pixie dust on my brain for the past few weeks.

It's genius, really. A beautiful, sparkly dust that adds magic to any situation? Yes, please!

My daughter walks around with her pixie dust pouch around her neck as the two kids play "Jake" most afternoons. Encounter a problem? No worries, she's got the pixie dust. Come up against a villain? Have no fear, the pixie dust is right here!

But us adults, we've lost our ability to believe in the magic. We've let life and stale faith rob us of truly believing the unbelievable. We talk of having faith and having trust as we walk through life—with all its difficulties and challenges. We talk of "believing" as we scale walls and climb mountains of doubt, fear, adversity and ambition.

But what of the supernatural . . . of the magic that can be added to every situation?

I think we've lost our ability to truly believe because we've put our faith and our trust solely in the hands of God. We've given Him his rightful place of King in our life but we've left it at that. "God is in control. It's up to Him now," we confess in an attitude of defeat rather than spiritual surrender. Because if we remove our hands and our heart from that which we are hoping for, we remove ourselves from the risk of disappointment if it doesn't turn out the way we'd like and we can easily blame God or simply settle that it "wasn't His will."

But where is the magic in that?

There is no beauty in a hands-off hope. Though we cannot usurp the power of God, get in His way, or begin to fully understand His ways, we can take an active role in the story he is writing all around us. We can apply our beautiful, spirit-led, supernatural sparkle to every situation.

So what's your pixie dust?

What is it that you can sprinkle on the world around you?

What is it that you can bring to the struggling and the hurting in your life?

What beautiful light can you shine on the villains you come in contact with daily?

How can you engage in the hope you hold in your heart beyond placing it in the hands of God?

We've been given a gift in the Spirit to know when to step back and let God be God and when to play an active role in our story. We've been given unique gifts within ourselves as well, beauty that only we can bring to life.

What's your pixie dust?

Friend, the world needs your magic. The world needs your beautiful, sparkly dust. If you don't yet know what that is in your life, find out. There is buried treasure deep within all of us just waiting to be shared. And when we finally let it go, we'll watch ourselves and those around us take flight.

Do you know what unique beauty you bring to your life and the lives of those around you or do you need to dig in to find out what it is?

Prayer

Dear Heavenly Father, thank you that you love us at every point along our journey – you delight in us and in our children as we grow into physical, relational and spiritual maturity. Give us the courage to share our "pixie dust" with those whom you've placed in our lives. Shine through us, we pray. In Jesus' Name, Amen.

SEVEN

Feeling Like You've Blown It?

Cindi McMenamin

If any of you lacks wisdom, you should ask God, who gives generously to all without finding fault, and it will be given to you.

James 1:5 (NIV)

Do you ever have those days when you feel like you've blown it as a mom? I remember saying out of frustration to my teenager, "I don't know how to parent a teenager—I've never done it before!" (Now that must have made her feel real secure, huh? Or it made her feel like she had an edge.)

We all feel like we've blown it at times—as moms, as wives, as daughters, as employees, as friends. In fact, I believe nearly all of us carry guilt on our shoulders in some area of life, feeling that we have failed to measure up to others' standards . . . or our own. I will be the first to tell you that I've failed more times than I'd like to count. In fact, in my book, *When a Mom Inspires Her Daughter*, I talk about more of my failures as a mom than my victories. That's because we can learn

21

through our mistakes. We can be shaped by our mistakes. And we can become more humble and extend more grace toward others when we are able to recognize the areas in which we have needed God's grace, wisdom, and correction.

If you are feeling that you are not measuring up, wherever you are in life, let me reassure you with this:

1. You are not where you are by chance. If you are the mom of a daughter—or son (or both)—don't think for a moment that took God by surprise. During the course of your mothering, God at no point regretted making you a mom. Psalm 18:30 says that "God's ways are perfect," and therefore, He makes no mistakes.

2. You can still be used for God's purposes. In Scripture, we find these wonderful words written by the Psalmist that describe our significance and our destiny, in the hands of an all-knowing, all-seeing God:

My frame was not hidden from you when I was made in the secret place. When I was woven together in the depths of the earth, your eyes saw my unformed body. All the days ordained for me were written in your book before one of them came to be (Psalm 139:15-16).

That verse tells me that you and I were planned out, intricately designed, and then placed where we are for purposes that we might not realize at the moment. So even if you're struggling with where you are in life, that didn't take God by surprise, either. Offer to Him all that you have and don't have. At times He can use you more in your humility and weakness than if you were a superstar, thinking you were doing just fine without Him.

3. You can receive God's wisdom, just by asking. I have been particularly encouraged lately by James 1:5 which says:

If any of you lacks wisdom, you should ask God, who gives generously to all without finding fault, and it will be given to you.

Did you catch that? God gives wisdom generously (He's not stingy in doling out the wisdom), He gives to all (even you, and even if you feel you don't deserve it), and He gives without finding fault (meaning He won't say "Uh no, gave it to you before and you didn't use it").

Feeling like you're blowing it? Take it to the Generous One who knows all about it and is waiting for you to seek His wisdom and His ear.

Prayer

Dear Heavenly Father, sometimes I feel like I blow it in some unique way—like my flaws and failures in parenting are somehow worse than others' are. Thank you for your grace that meets me at my point of need. Help me give myself grace, too. In Jesus' Name, Amen.

EIGHT

If I Have Not Love

Jill McSheehy

If I had the gift of being able to speak in other languages without learning them and could speak in every language there is in all of heaven and earth, but didn't love others, I would only be making noise. If I had the gift of prophecy and knew all about what is going to happen in the future, knew everything about everything, but didn't love others, what good would it do? Even if I had the gift of faith so that I could speak to a mountain and make it move, I would still be worth nothing at all without love. If I gave everything I have to poor people, and if I were burned alive for preaching the Gospel but didn't love others, it would be of no value whatever.

I Corinthians 13:1-3 (NLT)

The alarm sounded at 6:52 Saturday morning. I had hoped to view the lunar eclipse but I missed it somehow. Already awake, I brewed myself coffee and settled in my chair. Drew, my eight-year-old, stumbled out and covered himself with a blanket on the couch. I opened my Bible to the passage in the day's devotional. As I was reading, Alyssa, age four, hobbled out of her room and sat beside me, snuggling in the early morning stillness.

Quiet Reflection

I cherished the moment. My children, quiet and still with the innocence of the morning, led me to contemplate. The past few days I'd been begging God to help me be a better mom. In constant pain with my back and my husband working long hours, I'd found myself short-tempered with them. I also recognized how many good habits I've let slide recently, from our morning devotions to our weekly do-some-thing-for-another day.

In the stillness of the morning, gazing upon my two precious gifts, a quiet thought came to me. *Only one thing is necessary.*

If I Have Not Love

My mind drifted to the familiar passage of 1 Corinthians 13, the part prior to what is dubbed as the "Love Chapter," and I began to imagine . . .

If I read eloquent devotionals every morning with my children, but do not have love, I am a sounding gong or a clanging cymbal . . .

If I have the gift of teaching, and impart wisdom to my children at every teachable moment, and can answer every Bible question, and if I never experience angst over my children's souls because my unwavering faith is in God alone, but do not have love, I am nothing . . .

And if I involve my children in every volunteer opportunity available and teach them to give sacrificially, and if I work my body into exhaustion trying to do everything possible for their benefit, but do not have love, I gain nothing . . .

Super [Christian] Mom Fallout

As an overachiever, I tend to put a lot of pressure on myself to do everything and be everything for my children. Yet most of the time my efforts lead to

(1) exhaustion,

(2) guilt over not measuring up, and

(3) impatience with the kids when they don't fit my expectations.

Where is the love in that?

Of course I love my children. But does my tone of voice communicate love? Do they feel loved by the way I voice my frustration with the Pop-Tart crumbs on the floor . . . again? Deep down, do they believe I love being on time more than cherishing them as we rush out the door? Does my exasperation at one. more. story at bedtime show that they are more important than my desire to turn in my mommy-badge for the evening?

The Greatest of These

My prayer became, "Help me love them and show them love." And maybe that means laying off the guilt I feel for missing morning devotionals with them or serving every week or reading the Bible together every night. Perhaps in my quest to incorporate all the good things into their childhood, all that's left is a cranky mom who has missed the point.

May I remember that above anything I do, say, provide, or train, "the greatest of these is love" (1 Cor. 13:13b). And deep in my soul I know that when love is the center, the foundation, the everything-love, the greatest thing—will propel us to do the good things.

Prayer

Father, help me to remember that the greatest thing I can do for my children is love them well. Help me to let go of guilt, exhaustion, or exasperation at the things I have failed to do and turn instead to the task of showing them your love by loving them well myself.

NINE

Childlike Faith:
Praying for a Puppy

Kristan Dooley

Then Jesus called the children over to him and said to the disciples, "Let the little children come to me! Never send them away! For the Kingdom of God belongs to men who have hearts as trusting as these little children's . . ."

Luke 18:16 (NLT)

Last year, on our way home from vacation, God told me to get a puppy for my girls. I promise you, He did. I know it was Him because I would never get a puppy for anyone. Cute as they may be (as puppies), I don't like dogs. I don't do pets. They just aren't my thing. I have successfully managed to kill three beta fish since my youngest has been born and before that, as a newlywed, I accidently dropped our beta down the garbage disposal one day. Went to turn on the light switch and, believe it or not, I flipped the disposal on instead. I quickly turned it off and called Dave to see if he thought it was dead!

I am not good for them. They are not good for me. But there lives in my house an adorable seven-year-old who has an intense love for

28

dogs. She goes to her grandma's house to visit Maggie, her best friend (an eight-year-old Maltese). For about two years Addilyn prayed daily for a dog and I proceeded to buy her every stuffed, electronic, walking, sitting, barking dog they put out on toy shelves.

But her sweet little prayers reached her Father in Heaven and He instantly got to work. He told her to ask for whatever she wanted. She believed, she asked, she pleaded, relentlessly, consistently, and it worked. He heard her prayers and He turned my ear.

Jesus told me to buy a dog (you can try that on your spouse next time if you want). It worked for us. Dave thought I was crazy, but he also knows that when I feel the Father asking me to do something it will eventually get done.

One our way home from Florida we took a brief detour to pick up Addy's Morkie (Maltese/Yorkie) puppy. She was eight weeks old and anxiously awaiting the arrival of her new owner.

Here's where it gets good. *Addy didn't know.* We told her we were stopping by someone's house so Daddy could help them with something. We walked into this house, Addy immediately picked up her puppy and then she didn't believe us.

"Are you kidding?" she cried. "Tell the truth!"

You know, this is just like me. I serve a good God. He is a great dad and He has amazing things in store for me. He has given me big dreams and sometimes I hesitate to believe in them because I think to myself, "Surely He's kidding."

God doesn't play with our hearts. That's not His character. If He has put something in there, then we can believe in it. If we have asked Him, then we can trust him. He isn't kidding. His promises are true.

Prayer

Give me that childlike faith, Jesus. The faith to believe everything you say regardless of the circumstances around me. Thanks for being a good dad. Thanks for having good things for me. Thanks for hearing and answering the prayers of our hearts.

TEN

When Busyness Stings Like a Bee

Christina Caro

Come to Me, all you who labor and are heavy laden, and I will give you rest.

Matthew 11:28 (NKJV)

It happened while we were driving home the other night.

I had picked up my daughters, five and seven, from their first night of arts camp at our church. We had screeched in a minute late only an hour and a half earlier, after we had waited for my husband to arrive to take over with our toddler. So we had accomplished baths and dinner and cleaning the kitchen and "dance hair" and made it to camp. While they danced, I had run to Trader Joe's to stock up on the things we'd run out of over our long weekend away.

Their eyes danced with excitement as they breathlessly told me about their first night. Mirabella had a *real* ballerina for a teacher and wanted to teach me all the steps, right there in the sanctuary; her

31

younger sister, Emerie, wanted to know if we could go for ice cream. "Yes," I said, as I clumsily mirrored Mirabella's moves.

Emerie jumped up and down. I smiled at my ability to say, "yes." I don't say it often enough, and I hate it.

They talked excitedly through dessert, about new friends and what they were learning. For some reason, as we turned into our neighborhood, Mirabella made a comment about porcupines. "You know," I said, "sometimes Emerie reminds me of a porcupine. Because she's very cute and sweet, but when she gets mad, she can get kind of prickly." I looked back at Emerie to see how this made her feel, and she gave me a self-aware thumbs up.

"Deal," she said.

We talked about how Mirabella can be a bit of a sloth; she likes to take her time and is deliberate about all that she does.

"What animal would I be?" I asked.

"A cheetah," Emerie said, "running around everywhere."

"A bee," Mirabella said quickly. "Because you're always busy and running around cleaning something."

Sucker punch.

While Daniel and I had brunch during our getaway the previous weekend, my eyes had welled with tears. Over a fistful of months, we'd been dealing with a lot of meltdowns, a lot of unchecked emotion, behavioral issues without clear solutions, and I finally had the distance there to evaluate my role in it.

"Ever since we've had three," I said carefully, "they are not getting the one-on-one attention they deserve. I haven't learned to manage all the things that have to be done *and* spend quality time with them. I know other people do. I just haven't." We talked about how the work can't just be left undone – if we only go on adventures, the laundry will pile up, the house will be cluttered and dirty, stressing us all out, the tomatoes will rot on the vine – there *are* jobs that just must be done.

"I feel like part of my calling in this season is to cultivate a home that we *want* to be in. This is the backdrop of our children's memories, and I want it to be comfortable; I want it to be a haven. I want you to breathe a sigh of relief when you walk in the door."

"I get that," he said, "but we haven't worked as hard as we have for you to come home just to clean. That's not what I'm *still* working so hard for. When I come home and ask about your day, sure it's nice to see things clean. But I get much happier when I hear about what you've all done together."

My eyes filled with tears. He was right.

We are very fortunate in this season to be able to sacrifice in other areas to afford the occasional house cleaning. Previously, we had used it as a reset, every couple months. The kind but pushy woman always jockeys for us to increase her frequency. You know, to save us $20 per cleaning. Of course this doesn't make financial sense, but it's not just about money.

Having our home cleaned twice per month feels like a slap in the face to me, like an indictment on my ability to keep our home well. Cleaning our house feels like something I'm *supposed* to do, since I'm not bringing in money right now, and since I'm here most days.

But then our children called me a busy bee. And they weren't wrong.

"What animal would Daddy be?" I had asked them, stung.

"He would be a bee too, but he'd also be part giant panda. Because pandas keep healthy and strong by playing, and Daddy is playful."

"I don't play?" I asked.

"Well, not really," Mirabella said.

So, we are spending the money in this season. I am still uncomfortable about it. But Daniel says, "You are the only person who can mother our children. Anyone can clean our house."

I am so grateful for a husband who loves and sees us so clearly in this way. I'm grateful for the resources that haven't always been there, that may not always be there, but that we have available right now to make this happen.

So now we're going adventuring. Maybe it will only be in a blanket fort or out in the backyard. But I am going to work on correcting my course. On looking up, paying attention, listening patiently, and saying the important "yes" as often as I can.

"Mommy, can you watch me dance?" *Yes.*

"Mommy, play in the pool with me!" *Yes.*

"Mommy, can you help me with this puzzle?" *Yes.*

I am working on correcting my course. On looking up, paying attention, listening patiently, and . . .

Maybe, for you, it's not about cleaning the house. I don't know what it is that keeps you from being fully present for your kids or from saying yes more often. Take some time to ask the Lord to show you where you need to slow down and soak up this season. Ask Him what tasks and responsibilities you need to exchange for adventure and connection with your kids. Then wait as He shows you the strategy to change your course.

Anyone can {insert daunting life task here} . . . but only *we* can mother our children. This may not always mean we can give up said task . . . but it can remind us to lay it aside when our kids need to be top priority. This is a dance in itself and it's one we will continue to learn and re-choreograph each season of our lives.

What animal would your kids say you are? If it's not the one you want, what can you do in this season to change their perspective?

Prayer

Heavenly Father, you model this peaceful, present kind of parenting perfectly. Thank you for your grace that meets us right where we are. Give us 'busy bees' gentle reminders throughout our day to be present and engaged with where you have us in each stage of life and motherhood. Help us to prioritize well and to forgive ourselves when we miss the mark. In Jesus' Name, Amen.

ELEVEN

Overcoming the Temptation of Insecurity

Varina Denman

*Do not be afraid, little flock, for your Father has been pleased to give you
the kingdom.*

Luke 12:32 (NLT)

School was my first experience out from under the shelter of my
mother's wings. Since I was a mommy's girl, it took me a while
to recover from separation anxiety, and even longer to fit in with the
other first graders. But soon I realized that when I completed an assignment, my teacher was pleased, thereby recreating the sense of
safety I had left at home.

Mrs. Hallowell hung a poster on the front wall just next to the
dusty chalkboard, and every student's name was neatly written down
the left side. For every book read, she would place a gold foil star next
to the student's name. Before long, my row of stars stretched way past

the others, and the teacher praised me in front of the class. That row of foil stars gave me confidence in myself.

Even though I was timid and shy, I *perceived* that my abilities proved I was worth something, and I felt good about ME. Little did I know I was developing a bad habit. Even though the teacher's intention was merely to nurture a love of reading (which she did), I also learned to seek praise for my accomplishments instead of dealing with insecurity in a healthy manner.

In fourth grade, I became Mrs. Baughman's "teacher's pet" because I was the quietest student among a rowdy group. In seventh grade I won first chair in the orchestra, beating out the eighth and ninth graders. In high school, I excelled in academics and graduated valedictorian of my class. And with each of these achievements came a boost to my confidence, reminding me that I was something special—the one with foil stars by my name. It wasn't until I left college, married, and had children that those hypothetical gold stars began to tarnish.

At that time, I was home with my kids all day long, and there was no one passing out awards. Even though I had wanted to become a mommy ever since I crawled out from under my own mother's wing, the mundane tasks associated with housework shook my self-esteem. My husband praised me for the love I showered on our little ones, but it didn't feel the same, and I began to doubt my worth. Those bad habits I had accidentally fallen into as a child began to take their toll, and I realized I was giving in to the sin of insecurity.

All women yearn for worth and value, but we become unhealthy when we look for it in the wrong places.

For me, it was the temptation to lean on my own accomplishments, my behavior, even my appearance, instead of leaning on God and His promises. Through much prayer and Bible study—not to mention the example set by a slew of spiritually-mature friends and family—I began to realize that God alone holds the key to granting self-esteem. When I put my worth in Christ instead of my own accomplishments, I have value each and every day. God may have created me quiet and shy—a full-blown introvert—but he made me that way deliberately with a plan in mind. He gave me talents, but they weren't intended solely for my benefit. After all, human accomplishments can disappear in a flash, and they're meaningless compared to the fulfillment that comes from knowing the Lord. And that's the reason He gave me those gifts in the first place: to serve HIM.

It's been forty-two years since I earned that string of gold stars in Mrs. Hallowell's class, but I still struggle with the temptation of seeking worldly pursuits to make up for my insecurity. I must continually remind myself that God is forever faithful to His promises, and He's all the security I need. As a child of the King, I am treasured. I've been given purpose, and I am loved and accepted. All I need to do is get out of His way and trust Him to love me as much as He said He would.

Prayer

Heavenly Father, thank you for loving me so well. Help me to receive your love for me in childlike trust as I learn how to trust what you say about me. Grant me the wisdom to pass along this kind of trust to my children so that they, too, will find their foundation of security strongly rooted in you. In Jesus' Name, Amen.

TWELVE

It Isn't Even 7 a.m. Yet

Heather James

You made me; you created me. Now give me the sense to follow your commands.

Psalm 119:73 (NLT)

It isn't yet 7 a.m. and they're beating each other with Wii sports attachments. Sure, they're made of foam, but I know they'll manage to make the blows hurt nonetheless.

I only wanted to sit on the couch and drink my coffee, but their epic battle pushes me into the kitchen to stand and watch and pray.

Dear Lord, I pray for my crazy, bat-crazy but utterly wonderful sons. I pray that they would not hurt each other, not hurt me, not hurt the dog, the cat, the walls, or the floors. I pray that in Your infinite wisdom You will find a purpose and reason in their adult lives, a good one, a great one, for all the practice they squeeze into a day with their epic gladiator battles.

Lord, now I'm watching them play lion tamer and lion. My youngest is getting whipped but he doesn't seem to mind. Thank you for making them with thick skin and high tolerances for pain so that they're able to take a blow here and there—and apparently a good whipping, too—while still letting their imaginations run wild and free in the world around them.

(Prayer pause for child's tears. One whip too many. Kisses, then a full turnover of all weapons.)

Lord, please continue to give me the strength to deal with some of their behavior, which is not natural, nor even sane to me as a mother.

I know this play is necessary, within reason. I know that when little boys get to explore who they are, and then, with a mother's watchful eye, go on to explore the delicate line between play and too much, they'll become men who will stand up to fight when the time comes. And also men who exhibit mercy as necessary.

I realize that little boys, especially at this age, are born with a natural inclination to be gladiators and lion tamers, but only a mother can show them how to nonetheless respect the lion.

Thank You, God, for giving me sons. (Even though I only wanted to drink my coffee in peace.)

Prayer

Thank you, God, for the gift of my children. Thank you for creating each child with his and her own unique personality, talents, and desires. Please help me to encourage those gifts which you have given them, and give me wisdom in correcting and redirecting the behaviors that don't serve them well. In Your Name, Amen.

THIRTEEN

Surrendered

Alison Everill

Nor height, nor depth, nor any other created thing, will be able to separate us from the love of God, which is in Christ Jesus our Lord.

Romans 8:39 (NASB)

R ight now I am sitting in my living room. The sky is just beginning to dim (I love this time of day), my three little boys are giggling in their bedroom, and my husband is walking in the door safe and sound. I am smiling because this moment is a snapshot of God's great grace in my life. I don't deserve any of what I am experiencing right now, yet somehow, I am being lavished upon by the One who loves me most.

As I think back over the last few weeks I really feel a sense of gratitude. It's been so much fun. I've been able to cut a demo, go to a songwriters' conference, and lead a night of praise and worship at my home church. These are all dreams fulfilled. I am so thankful that the Lord allows me to do what I love the most to honor Him. What could be better?

Over the last six months things have changed drastically for my family. My husband, after pastoring for nearly twenty years, felt the Lord moving Him from ministry into the secular business world. Talk about a crazy time! We have been hanging on waiting for the Lord to open doors, windows, or even a doggie door! He has kept us in the dark, forcing us to trust Him. Imagine that! Trust God? Really? It has been a time for us to put our money where our mouth is, and God has been faithful. I watch Him daily bring my frantic heart back to the rock-solid truth of Scripture and cause me to truly believe Him when He says that nothing can separate me from the love of God which is in Christ Jesus (Romans 8:39).

I am learning daily to surrender my will and my plans to the Father's desires for me—to make His desires my own. There is great peace in that. I still have many "freak out" moments as I wait on the Lord, but I feel myself growing, and as the Apostle Paul said, "For momentary light affliction is producing for us an eternal weight of glory far beyond all comparison" (2 Cor. 4:16). This isn't all there is. In fact, the things we run from, pray against, cry and agonize over are most often things that the Lord is trying to use to bring us closer to Him.

So, with fear and trembling I pray . . .

Prayer

. . . Lord, I am willing to be in the storm if that's where You are.

FOURTEEN

Jesus Restores

Cheryl Lutz

And I will restore to you the years that the locusts have eaten.

Joel 2:25 (KJV)

I was standing in the fitting room gazing into the mirror contemplating my choice, when the voice of my teenage daughter interrupted my thoughts. "Did you find one, Mom?" I affirmed; then her next words rocked my little fitting room world. "Well, let me see!"

Gulp!

She seriously wanted to see it. I regretfully admit that this was one of the first shopping trips we had ever gone on together without angry words being tossed back and forth. But this day had been different. My firstborn girl and I were having a beautiful time at the mall together.

I didn't want to alter the mood, so I sheepishly opened the door. To our mutual horror, her face melted before my eyes as she screamed, "Eww . . . *not on!*" I quickly closed the door feeling mortified as I heard giggling coming from the surrounding rooms.

She is now twenty-four years old, and we laugh hysterically about the day I opened the fitting room door shirtless, to show her the bra I had chosen. We also rejoice in the fact that we are now close friends.

Dear Ones, it was not always like this. We allowed worlds to collide with my fashion-loving girl and our fishbowl existence as a Pastor's family.

I confess many times I objected to her clothing based more on what others might think rather than personal and biblical convictions. I allowed Satan to drive a wedge between one of my children and me.

Do you fight with your teens about clothing? Are your convictions based on biblical principles or are they more about fear of what others think?

Stop and pray now for wisdom. Open the lines of communication and ask for forgiveness for ungodly responses. Explain the beauty and blessing of honoring our Heavenly Father in all things, including our clothing. Make sure the bottom line is about glorifying Him, and not primarily about trying to meet others' expectations.

Like me, have you allowed the locusts (our enemy) to eat precious years with your children? Take heart! As we seek His face and obedience to His word he fulfills His promise to: "Restore the years the locusts have eaten!"

What He has done for my girl and me, He will do for you too!

Prayer

Dear Heavenly Father, I ask for wisdom to know how to navigate these 'gray areas' of parenting and thank you for making forgiveness so readily and freely available to me when I miss the mark. I ask that you for wisdom for my children as well as they learn to make these choices for themselves as they mature. In Jesus' Name, Amen.

FIFTEEN

Freedom

Lori Kennedy

An inheritance quickly gained in the beginning will not be blessed at the end.

Proverbs 20:21 (NIV)

With upcoming elections, I see so many things about the goals of the different candidates and parties and what they believe and stand for. It is easy to see the division. However, I recently ran across a quote that allowed me to see how much we are all alike in our desires and how those desires in many cases, although good, don't produce healthy results in the long run.

Let me explain. You see, I find that it's not about which party you're for, it's about becoming who God made you to be. Romans 5:3-4 says that we should "rejoice in our sufferings, because we know that suffering produces perseverance; perseverance, character; and character, hope." The hope for our future comes from our willingness to know that it isn't always an easy road and besides taking responsibility, we may have to work and fight for what's important to us.

I believe on some level that in my desire for my children to have "easy" lives, I have rescued them from suffering and done too much for them in the name of protection. They have not always had to take responsibility for their actions.

Let me give you an example:

I didn't have a lot of great memories from my childhood. For my boys to have good memories has been a hot button for me all their lives. I have found myself overlooking a punishment in the name of creating a memory; case in point—letting them off of being grounded for one night to go to Homecoming. *By the same token, I have personally chosen not to suffer at times because rescuing them was easier for me.* I took away their ability to learn responsibility because I chose the easier road, still in the name of protecting my children.

There have been times, for example, that I would find out at the last minute that a paper was due the next day. I would stay up late with my child helping them complete the paper. That, in itself, was not letting them suffer their own consequences. However, I even went a step further. Because it was the easier road, I would sometimes write portions of that paper for them as I was tired and waiting on them to do it on their own was harder for me. I can see that in this desire to protect them, I have actually done them a great disservice. Because of the lack of responsibility needed and suffering required by them, I must now ask myself if I have not allowed them the opportunity to produce the perseverance and character needed to keep hope alive for their future.

Our pilgrim ancestors came to this country not even knowing what they might encounter, but I don't believe for one minute that they didn't think it would be a challenge. They had to re-create their homes, their careers, their very lives from scratch. They were willing to work hard and take responsibility, as well as many risks, in order to see freedom prevail. They felt that the sacrifices were worth the hope for their (and for your) future. Not only did they think past themselves, but they even thought past their children and selflessly gave to society as a whole, knowing that creating a whole new country wouldn't be a walk in the park.

So read the quote below and ask God how He would have you sow into your children's lives today. I'm convicted that I've given too much in the name of protection and not allowed my children to take responsibility and to learn and fight for what they want on their own. My desire was a good one—protection of my children—and quite honestly a desire I think everyone agrees upon no matter which political party you may support. However, as you can see below, we could possibly be stealing the very freedom of those we are trying to protect by allowing them to think, through our overprotection of them, that their whole life will be easy. Sometimes our view of what's best and God's view of what's best do not completely match up, as we can only see what's right in front of us whereas God sees the whole picture—past us, past our children and into all future generations.

Here is a quote about the fall of Athens, Greece, by the historian Edward Gibbon:

"In the end, more than freedom, they wanted security. They wanted a comfortable life, and they lost it all—security, comfort, and freedom. When the Athenians finally wanted not to give to society but for society to give to them, when the freedom they wished for most was freedom from responsibility, then Athens ceased to be free and was never free again."

Here's another quote by the poet and novelist George Santayana: *'Those who don't remember the past are condemned to repeat it."*

I have seen that my desire for my children has been security and a comfortable life. Those things aren't wrong. However, in my quest for that, have I taken away their willingness to accept responsibility and ultimately, their freedom because I've done too much for them in the name of love and not allowed them to navigate their own way even through times of suffering?

Prayer

Dear Heavenly Father, nothing in my life offers me more opportunities to exercise my trust in you like being a mother does. I pray for myself and for my children that we will be people of confidence in you and that we will be found faithful in our generation. In Jesus' Name, Amen.

SIXTEEN

Jesus Did Not Parent Toddlers

Tricia Williford

And He said to me, 'My grace is sufficient for you, for My strength is made perfect in weakness."

2 Corinthians 12:9a (NKJV)

In his perfect holiness, Jesus did not do what I have done today. **Today sucked.**

Forgive me if you do not like that term. But it did. No way around it. My boys were disobedient and whiny. I was out of patience and fortitude. We were plain sick of each other. This house (and the surrounding parks) were not big enough for the three of us. There was yelling, whining, snapping, and crying, among all parties. I did not behave as I would have hoped. But neither did they. I called in reinforcements. Friends prayed for me.

I bought—and pleasurably drank—a mocha.

And I called on all the Scripture I could recall to please, please, get me through the morning. Carry me to nap time. And that's when it suddenly occurred to me: Jesus did not parent toddlers. Yes, he withstood and refused temptations of many kinds, of his eyes, his stomach, his flesh. But of all the paths he walked that are ours as well, he was not the stay-at-home parent of preschoolers. When he escaped the throngs and pursued solitude with his Father, he did not have to arrange for childcare. When he fasted, he did not have to prepare meals for picky eaters.

"Let the little children come to me," he said. But he could send them home when he was finished teaching them. And when they fell into tantrums in his presence, I'm pretty sure their mothers swooped in to avoid a public scene.

"Be holy as I am holy." In his holiness, he did not do the day-in-day-out *constantness* of arguing, negotiating, potty training, timeouts, scraped knees, lessons in sharing, and weary exhaustion with their little sinful natures.

But he did give these children to me.

And he ordained today.

And his grace is sufficient.

(And they are sleeping now. *Thank you, Lord.*)

Prayer

Dear Heavenly Father, thank you for your grace—sufficient, sustaining grace—that faithfully meets me at my point of need. Thank you for reminding me that my role is not to be a perfect mom, but to be a humble daughter who trusts in you. In Jesus' Name, Amen

SEVENTEEN

Welcoming Guests

Dorothy Johnson

Do not forget to entertain strangers, for by so doing some have unwittingly entertained angels.

Hebrews 13:2 (NKJV)

Read Luke 7:36 – 49.

Have you ever noticed how important eating is in the Bible? The Proverbs 31 woman rises early to prepare food for her family. Sarah cooked a feast for the three travelers who dropped in with mind-blowing news (Gen. 17).

Much scripture is devoted to Jesus' last meal with his disciples. Because it embodies his sacrifice, he instructed them to remember and observe the breaking of bread and pouring of wine forever (Luke 22). Communal meals were part of the new church in Acts (see Chapter 3). In the same way, we still enjoy potlucks with our church congregations and at friends' houses.

While food is often at the center of our gatherings, hospitality embodies much more than just eating a meal together. Remember how Abraham brought water for his visitors to wash their feet. Then there was the Pharisee who didn't offer such a courtesy to Jesus at the dinner where the woman anointed him and washed his feet with her tears (Luke 7).

True hospitality is the opening of our hearts to one another, saying you are important enough for me to go all out for your visit. With really close friends, it often involves cooking and cleaning up together amidst lots of laughter.

However, sometimes it isn't convenient to entertain—even when it comes easy to you. I observed that with my parents. They definitely had the gift of hospitality and loved having people in for a meal or just coffee and dessert. Mother made it look easy; although now I realize there were times folks dropped in unannounced when she was tired to the bone.

One example of their long-suffering involved one of Mother's older brothers, who lived in a bordering state. More than once, we looked out the window as his car rolled up in front of the house. No phone call, no letter—just a big grin as we opened the door to find him and my aunt standing there.

When we were young, my brother and I loved to see them arrive. He always had pockets-full of nickels, dimes and quarters to drop into our hands. Sometimes he bought T-bone steaks that he cooked for us.

My mother worked full time, but I can remember her voicing her exasperation only once as we peered out to see their car at the curb. I suppose my uncle's freedom to drop in unannounced to see his baby sister is a testament to her love and acceptance of him and my aunt. Now that I'm an adult who has worked, it wears me out just thinking about those visits. Even though I inherited some of their hospitality genes, I'm not sure I could do the same without complaining, but it would probably be later.

I'm proud of my parents' legacy of hospitality. I hope I will always be ready to share what I have—both food and the Good News—with whoever shows up at my door. After all, that's the way the Lord greeted me many years ago when He called into His heavenly family.

Prayer

O Lord, remind me of your unfailing patience when I'm faced with inconvenience. Help me to pour out upon others the abundant grace you have shown me. In Jesus' Name, Amen.

EIGHTEEN

Stones, a Journal, and Faith

Jennifer Vander Klipp

*For in the gospel a righteousness from God is revealed, a righteousness that
is by faith from first to last, just as it is written:
"The righteous will live by faith."*

Romans 1:17 (NIV)

On the mantle in my living room are two small stones. One has
a picture of a house drawn on it. The other has the name of
my son, Joshua, and his birth date. I could have many more stones up
there than the mantle could hold, but these two are significant. These
stones remind me of difficult times in my life when God was faithful.
When I feel myself get anxious or start to worry about how God will
resolve a situation, I look at these stones.

The very essence of the Christian life is faith. To even become a
Christian requires faith in Jesus as our Savior. To continue to grow as
a Christian requires our faith to grow. In James 1:2-4 it says, "Consider it pure joy, my brothers, whenever you face trials of many kinds,

because you know that the testing of your faith develops perseverance. Perseverance must finish its work so that you may be mature and complete, not lacking anything" (NIV).

Testing is one of the ways God grows our faith. Remembering our past trials and how God was faithful to us through them will help us in future trials. One way to do this is to keep a prayer journal. Write down your prayers and then write down how God answers them. This is a great way to remember what God has done for you.

Sharing how God has answered your prayers with others is another way to encourage each other and to grow our faith. Small groups and Bible studies provide a great situation to share how God is working in your life. It's also encouraging to see what others are going through and how God has been faithful to them.

Finally, we need to be in the Word and in prayer daily. The more we know about God, the more we know we can trust Him. There's an old hymn that goes,

"Whisper a prayer in the morning.
Whisper a prayer at noon.
Whisper a prayer in the evening
To keep your heart in tune."

The more we are talking to God (and listening) through prayer, the closer we will stay to Him and be able to walk by faith and not by our circumstances. As you spend time with God, He will reveal to you the things He wants you to be doing. Do them. Sharing these things with others in your small group can help you become accountable and give you the strength to do what God wants you to do.

Take that step in faith and do what you know God wants you to do. As you obey Him and see how He is faithful to you, you will be encouraged to take more steps.

Prayer

Dear Heavenly Father, I pray for the wisdom to know what to do and the courage to do it, even when it is hard. In Jesus' Name, Amen.

NINETEEN

Are You a Huge, Huge Christian?

Linda Vujnov

. . . all of you, be like-minded, be sympathetic, love one another, be compassionate and humble.

1 Peter 3:8 (NLT)

My girlfriend has five boys. I'm told this is better than having five girls, but I suppose some would disagree. In addition to one girl, I have three boys. While our girl is happy watching movies and creating handmade gifts alone in her bedroom, the boys organize baseball games in our living room where couch cushions are makeshift bases, the sleeping dogs are the foul ball markers, and a paper towel roll and stuffed football serve as the bat and baseball. Boys do everything at high volume, high energy, and in perpetual motion, thus, my girlfriend ranks high on the chart of nominees for "most resilient and uber awesome."

One day while referencing her, and in the midst of conveying the fact that she is kind, fun to be around, and a great friend, our youngest stated that she was also a, "huge, huge Christian." Her acts of kindness, generosity, and the lack of the yelling gene conveyed to our boy that since her character reflected that of Jesus she wasn't simply a Christian, but a huge, huge, Christian.

After his comment, I couldn't help but question, "Do I reflect Jesus? Am I a huge, huge, Christian? The answer is: Not always, definitely, not always.

According to Socrates, "An unexamined life isn't worth living." If I want to be the person who Christ has called me to be, I need to not only do some self-examination, but I also need to make some changes. In order to exhibit character traits that reflect Jesus, I need to engage in self-reflection and self-control.

Admittedly, I am impatient, judgmental, and critical, which is not too Christ-like. As I recognize my character flaws, I also need to make a concerted effort to make visible changes, otherwise, I will remain the same and will continue to reveal my flagrant flaws to others.

So, what about you? Will you remain the same, or will others see the impact that God makes in your life because you project a Christ-like character?

I don't have any intention of remaining the same. I intend to strive for change, moment by moment through an intimate relationship with Jesus Christ. One day when someone asks our boy about me, I am hopeful that he will say, "I love my mom. She's a huge, huge, Christian."

Prayer

Dear Heavenly Father, may I remember that your desire is that my life reflect the life of Christ; and that you are always actively working in me to that end. Give me the grace to remember that what you want most from me is my trust, which will inevitably bring about spiritual maturity. In Jesus' Name, Amen.

TWENTY

Costly Deception

Shellie Rushing Tomlinson

Buy the truth and do not sell it.

Proverbs 13:23 (NIV)

When my sisters and I were teenagers we liked to play word games with our Mama. For instance, she might say, "Y'all sure are late getting home. What did y'all do after school?" It was a question we had little trouble answering truthfully. I mean, we did many things after school. For Mama's purposes, we'd pick out something that we knew she'd approve of like "Oh, we stopped by the library." We would neglect to mention that we never actually went inside the library. We just stopped by it, in the parking lot across the street to smoke Virginia Slims with the other cool kids.

The pressure, however, would begin to mount with each subsequent question. Staying in the game required us to proceed with caution, sort of like approaching an intersection with a flashing yellow light. Taking note of our distinct odor, unsuccessfully camouflaged with perfume, Mama might ask a more pointed question, "Have y'all been smoking?" While this type of question was more difficult, it was still doable. The way my sisters and I saw it, we may have at one time been smoking—but we had not been smoking, say . . . in the last ten minutes. That's usually when Mama would come back with the line guaranteed to strike fear in your heart, "Look me in the eyes, young lady, and tell me you haven't been smoking."

Uh-oh, decision time. The only thing worse than being caught breaking the Rushing Family Rules was lying about it. If the truth got you grounded, deception would get you something like five to ten in solitary!

Mama's lying lesson has a biblical foundation. The Lord exhorts us in Proverbs 13:23 to "buy the truth and never sell it." That word, "buy," deserves a closer look. No one coached my sisters and me on how to play those words games. We didn't have to be the brightest bulbs on the tree to figure out that telling the truth was going to cost us. But then, it still does, doesn't it? It's why we all find it tempting to fudge things at times, or dodge the issue like we girls did. If only we were as quick to acknowledge the flip side of that coin, that if we aren't truthful we'll cut ourselves off from the Lord's fellowship and His blessings!

Jesus is the Truth, and He can't bless a lie. The next time you have a choice to buy the truth or sell it, remember, "Truth might be costly, but none of us can afford deception."

Prayer

Dear Heavenly Father, may I be found faithful and true as I more and more often allow the Christ-life to live through me. Give me the strength to be honest, authentic and real—even when it hurts. In Jesus' Name, Amen.

TWENTY-ONE

When They Don't Love God Back

Jennifer O. White

*I urge you, first of all, to pray for all people. Ask God to help them;
intercede on their behalf, and give thanks for them.*

1 Timothy 2:1 (NLT)

D o you feel helpless watching your husband or one of your children resist the beautiful life God is offering? You know the joy of abiding and serving Him and you want them to know it too. You want them to want it, right?

Everything you've tried and hoped for may have failed. But God does not fail, and He invites you to partner with Jesus as an intercessor.

The Spirit intercedes for God's people in accordance with the will of God. Romans 8:27

He is sitting in the place of honor at God's right hand, pleading for us. Romans 8:34

I urge you, first of all, to pray for all people. Ask God to help them; intercede on their behalf, and give thanks for them. 1 Timothy 2:1

You have a VERY important role in this ministry of reconciliation. You are responsible for agreeing that God wants this and can do this.

Pray God's Word

Speaking God's truth out loud is a powerful weapon in the battle against the evil that ensnares the one we love. His Word is the Sword of His Spirit (Eph. 6:17). It has the power to slice away the slime of sin that blinds someone to God's gentleness, mercy and perfect love.

Faith believes that God is able to accomplish infinitely more than we can ask Him to do in the life of the one who is resisting Him (Eph 3:20). Faith prays believing that God's Word never returns void but always accomplishes His purposes (Isa. 55:11).

Praying God's Word over someone is a simple act of faith. It is a partnership with God's plan to save His people. Noah, who had never seen rain, built an ark because he trusted God. With your prayers, you are building an ark for your child or your husband.

When they don't love God back *yet*, you can pray the words of King David, a man after God's own heart. In Psalm 63, David affirms that nothing is more satisfying to him than God.

Prayer

Join me now in declaring that the truth of Psalm 63 will also be your child's and/or your husband's reality. When you do this, you are saying to God, "I believe You are able to move this mountain in _____'s life. I see it in my heart before I see it in my world." As you speak these words out loud, remember to listen for God's "Yes" and watch for His nod. His Spirit is agreeing with you and delighting that you want what He wants.

_____s soul will find no fulfillment in earthly things.
_____'s soul will long for You God. You are _____'s helper and _____ will know that well.

_____ will see Your power and Your glory and be satisfied.
_____ will know that You satisfy him/ her more than the richest feast.

_____ knows that Your love never fails him/her. _____ finds nothing in this world to compare with Your love.

_____ trusts You God and praises You day and night.
_____ s life is spent with lifted hands in praise and prayer to You God. _____ praises You with songs of joy.

_____ lies awake thinking of you, meditating on You through the night. _____ is captivated by Your majesty. His/her thoughts are always on You.

In the shadow of Your wing, _____ finds rest for his/her soul and sings songs of joy regardless of his/her circumstances. _____ clings to You.

Your strong right hand holds _____ securely. Every plan Satan has to destroy _____ will come to ruin because You, the Victorious God, are fighting for Him in the spiritual realm.

How do you feel after praying these things? Do you feel stronger? Celebrate!! God's Word is so powerful. Do you feel like this isn't quite right? Don't fret. Just lift your concern up to God and ask Him to reveal His truth about praying this way to you. He is your prayer coach and always ready to help you accomplish His will.

TWENTY-TWO

The Path of a Tornado

Anita Agers-Brooks

Though He slay me, yet will I trust Him. Even so, I will defend my own ways before Him.

Job 13:15 (NKJV)

She was exploring Paris the day a mother's worst fears became reality. As Debby played Parisian tourist, her family in Moore, Oklahoma, hunkered down. How could she know a monster approached back home?

On Monday, May 20, 2013, the twister swept businesses, homes, schools, cars, and human lives into its murderous dust. The sky darkened as a massive steel-blue wall cloud deepened its grip across the horizon. News agencies on television and radio implored the citizens skirting Oklahoma City's metropolitan and suburban areas to seek shelter immediately.

"Folks, this is not a tornado warning—it's a tornado emergency."

"Take cover underground."

"Do not get caught in your car. Do not hide under an overpass. The winds will accelerate and strengthen under bridges and highways."

People trembled as the funnel blasted across the earth, advancing toward heavily populated areas. The huge debris ball thickened in violent rotation. It tracked eastward and barreled closer to Debby's daughter, Jeany, leveling buildings as it bore down.

Children screamed. Dogs barked. Birds silenced. Men and women moved away from windows, hid their families in storm cellars and interior safe rooms, under mattresses in bathtubs, and beneath stairwells. Un-churched people prayed with faithful followers. *Fervently.*

In an interior closet, thirty-eight-year-old Jeany Marks Neely huddled with her sixteen-year-old son. "Pray, baby," were the last words Debby's daughter ever spoke. This is an excerpt of one of the true stories from my book, *Getting Through What You Can't Get Over.*

Debby Marks' daughter was killed by a cataclysmic natural event. You might expect a mother's bitterness. Who would fault her if she blamed God? But Debby staunchly refused. Like a female Job, she resolved to live courageously, even when the undeniable thinness between the wants of her body contrasted with those of her soul. In the path of a massive EF-5 tornado, Debby Marks made a decision not to give up her faith.

According to Debby, one of the ways she survives is to face her pain head-on. In *Getting Through,* I explore the Seven Stages of Grief, according to Jennie Wright, RN and Certified Grief Counselor. Each step requires we do the hard, right thing. We must feel, versus numbing out.

1. Shock and Denial
2. Pain and Guilt

3. Anger and Bargaining

4. Depression, Reflection, and Loneliness

5. The Upward Turn

6. Reconstruction and Working Through

7. Acceptance and Hope

By experiencing each, Debby is finding purpose in her pain. Yes, she has questions. Yes, her agony is torturous and raw. Yes, she wrestles with God. But she has learned to take off the mask, unfettered by protocol or political correctness, and like Job, express how she really feels.

In digging deep, Debby has also discovered the sweetness of surprising gifts. Sifting through the wreckage, words scrawled on yellowed fibers were found among the debris of Jeany's housea precious message from beyond the grave. Debby's fingers shook as she held the fragile piece of lined tablet paper. It said, "One task a day. Live, love, laugh. Keep silent. Keep God close. Love the boys."

In the path of a tornado, strengthened by a message of love, Debby is learning how to get through a loss she'll never get over. I hope her story helps you know your emotions are natural when blindsided by tragedy, fear, or betrayal. If you are stuck in a season of unresolved grief, find healing by picking up your feet and forcing them ahead.

My own motto verse is Job 13:15. *"Though He slay me, yet will I trust Him. Even so, I will defend my own ways before Him."*

Like Job, Debby, and me, I pray that no matter what happens, you never give up.

Prayer

Dear Heavenly Father, sometimes our losses feel completely overwhelming. Fill us with your Spirit, remind us of hope beyond the grave, and place within us a joy that allows us to smile—maybe even laugh a bit—when our hearts and minds are grieving. Give us the grace to sit with others in their grief and love them through us, we pray. In Jesus' Name, Amen.

TWENTY-THREE

Growing Up in Christ

Lisa Velthouse

Like newborn infants, long for the pure spiritual milk, that by it you may grow up into salvation—if indeed you have tasted that the Lord is good.

I Peter 2:2 (ESV)

We have a five-week-old in the house, so we are sleep-deprived and groggy-eyed. We are basketfuls of tiny baby clothes in the laundry room. We are pacifiers everywhere. We are hunger all the time. Between the little guy and me alone, there is always at least one person who wants to be eating.

***

A few nights ago, while my husband was away at work and some friends were visiting, the baby cried seemingly forever. But he had just eaten. He had a dry diaper too, and it was an hour past his usual bedtime, and this was his angry cry. I knew him well enough already to know he was trying to pull a power play—and this mama was determined not to be manipulated, and to help him learn the simple and basic skill of falling asleep instead.

Still, it was mind-numbing to sit there, listening to him like that. I've heard it said somewhere that an infant's cry has a physiological effect on a woman: specifically, it elicits a sense of actual panic in her. I can't say whether or not that claim is real science, but anecdotally I know it's true. Those tiny-lung shrieks can fry my nerves like nothing else, and more quickly too.

In my better moments, I like to think this whole cry/response thing is just one more example of God's brilliant design: take a new mom who's dog-tired from late-night feedings and physically beat-up from having given birth, and put something in her that makes her willingly rise and plod toward her child, to discover and to give what is needed, if for no other reason than to make the madness stop.

With that in mind, we come to 1 Peter 2:

Like newborn infants, long for the pure spiritual milk, that by it you may grow up into salvation—if indeed you have tasted that the Lord is good.

It occurred to me this week that the milk an infant longs for is directly tied to another being. Babies cannot simply crave the milk they need and then depend on themselves to get it. No, in this scenario, craving a thing is practically the same as craving its source. The baby cries, but there is no nourishment for him unless it is given by another.

The fact goes *unemphasized* in this passage, but when it comes to spiritual milk, the same underlying truth applies. We egocentric, we results-oriented, we self-sufficient types are prone to focus on our own accomplishments and efforts: the parts we bring to an equation.

We crave the spiritual milk, we consume the spiritual milk, we grow up in Christ as a result.

We are lining up to be presented with our applause, our award sashes, our shiny gold stars. But let's not forget that in this metaphor we are infants. In other words, not capable of much beyond basic re-flexes. In other words, there is an ever-giving Source at the beginning, middle, and end of this equation. He deserves the praise.

He has already, at the cross, exhausted Himself beyond a final breath, to give us what we need for complete forgiveness and lasting joy. It is our closeness to Him, drinking from all He pours out, that changes us. His food is how we are strengthened and how we are matured.

In Him we find, for starters: love that is steadfast, truth that's explosive, justice that captivates, mercy that overflows. We cannot take on qualities like these without absorbing His example of them first. For His is the only accurate example of them.

And we cannot expect to have the self-control and behavioral restraint that the rest of 1 Peter 2 talks about without qualities like these. Again, without His example. If spiritual milk is what we are to drink, the implication is there.

"If indeed you have tasted that the Lord is good"—wanting and needing to grow means wanting and needing, above all else, Him.

Prayer

Dear Heavenly Father, we admit to you our need for you – for you to fill us, for you to provide for us, for you to guide and direct us, for you to be with us. We acknowledge that we cannot do anything apart from you – and in the deepest part of who we are, we don't want to try! In Jesus' Name, Amen.

TWENTY-FOUR

How Do I Trust God More?

Sherri Sand

Trust God from the bottom of your heart;
don't try to figure out everything on your own.
Listen for God's voice in everything you do, everywhere you go;
he's the one who will keep you on track.

Proverbs 3:5-6 (The Message)

Is the act of believing a form of prayer?

As I prayed for my kids one day, I found myself grabbing for prayers. Fix-it prayers.

You see, my middle son has aspirations to play college basketball, and fear started speaking to me, "How will coaches find him in our small town of mountains and sage brush?"

My boat started taking on water fast. The more I prayed, the more anxiety I felt. Worry was grabbing the oars and paddling hard. So I lifted my oars out of the water and told God that I was more anxious now than before I started praying.

I sensed His wink and a reassuring, "I've got your boy."

71

My oar dipped toward the water's surface, "You sure?"

I felt God's laughter as He said, "I've got him. *I know the plans I have for him"* (Jeremiah 29:11).

I had somehow absorbed a negative belief about prayer when I was growing up. Difficulty would happen and the ladies in the church would promise to pray. But I didn't see victory through prayer. I saw disappointment and people clutching the edges of their hymnals every Sunday.

No one ever taught me this, but somehow I adopted the belief that God wouldn't be moved unless I prayed HARD. I thought fervency and frequency determined whether God would hear me. And any sin in me would decrease His desire to listen and undo all my hard work of praying. It seemed quite exhausting.

Walking in Faith

But through the years of listening to Graham Cooke and others, I've discovered the lie in that belief system. We don't have to beg God to meet our needs (Matthew 6:25-33). We don't carry the weight of responsibility for a particular outcome. Praying out of fear and worry won't accomplish anything. We deny God's character and His goodness when we operate out of worry.

God is saying to us, "Do you trust Me? Can you rejoice in My goodness through this difficulty? Can you connect with Me and gain perspective through My eyes? Can you let go of control and let Me meet your needs? Can you believe that I have your best in mind? Can you trust Me when My best for you and your best for you aren't in alignment?

"And if you can't trust yet, are you willing to let Me to reveal My goodness to you?" And we need to realize He's not saying that the difficulty in our lives is from Him. But He does promise to be with us and get us through it if we lean on His understanding and not our own (Proverbs 3:5).

I realized that my best prayer is to stand in a place of belief. Even if I don't say a word, my heart is smiling because I trust my heavenly Papa to do great things in my boy's life. My trust and belief open doors for God to work.

Fear and anxiety hinder what God can do in our lives—because we can't listen to God and fear at the same time. Fear shouts. God whispers.

And we step into control when we hold hands with fear and listen to its poison spread through our minds. Anxiety and fear leave us tossed in the waves. We can't see the shore and we become frightened. When we trust, we are open to what God is doing. Through intimacy and connection, we get a glimpse of His plans and we get to pray those plans into existence with Him (Romans 4:17).

Prayer

Father, stir and build my faith in you. I repent for unbelief. Take it far from me. I break agreements with the unbelief I've harbored. Some things are easy to trust you for. Others are like jumping off a cliff. I'm not there yet. Teach me your ways. Please reveal your goodness so I can walk in the freedom and joy You have for me. I want to walk free from fear and control, anxiety and worry. I want all you have for me. All those good things you established for me before the foundations of the world. Keep me in your peace and teach me to fight the enemy for control of my mind. In Jesus' Name, Amen!

TWENTY-FIVE

Little Children Come Unto Me

Jennie Atkins

Let the little children come to me, and do not hinder them, for the kingdom of God belongs to such as these.

Mark 10:14-15 (NIV)

Having just spent a long weekend with my newest granddaughter, who is not quite six months old, witnessing her boundless supply of happy smiles, and seeing the joy she gives my son and daughter-in-law, I naturally thought of the verse in Mark 10:14-15:

"Let the little children come to me, and do not hinder them, for the kingdom of God belongs to such as these."

Does this mean only children will enter through heaven's gates? I guess it's easy enough to explain away with the term child-like faith. But for me, it runs deeper.

Children have absolute trust. When my daughter was little, she would stand with her back to her dad and fall straight back into his arms—never looking back, never showing concern for her own safety, never doubting her father would catch her. As Christ's children, we should show the same level of trust for our Heavenly Father. He has our best interests in mind and knows us better than we know ourselves.

Kids have no fear. As my children grew up, they tried numerous activities to test their fate. They had no fear; nothing held them back from attempting the ridiculous--which often tested the condition of my heart and nerves more than it affected them. How many times have we wanted to do something, even felt God's prompting to move forward? Yet we stood cemented in place, buried in a myriad of doubts and fears, believing we'd be better off staying in our safe zone. If God ordains it, He has our back, our future, and our dreams.

Little ones are an endless supply of joy. Happiness radiates from them, nothing gets them down that can't be fixed with a hug or a little TLC. Adults, however, find themselves bogged down in the muck and the mire. The stress of everyday responsibilities zapping us of our joy. By turning our lives over to our creator, we've shared our load with The Almighty, the One who is able to heal us, comfort us, and provide for us. When we learn to trust in Him, he fills our hearts with His eternal joy.

Children have no worries. As we grow older, we worry about our next meal, the clothes on our backs, our jobs. We start each day with a to-do list. Children, on the other hand, tumble out of bed, greeting the day as if it were a new adventure—not drudgery. They'd even slip on the clothes they wore the previous day if we let them.

Being a child boils down to living in God's abundant grace. Knowing He will carry us in the hard times, rejoice over our good fortunes, be our alpha and omega, our comforter, our provider, our friend. Without Him, I am nothing. With Him, I can be the little child who runs into His arms when times are tough, who can worship Him with reckless abandon, and know that I am loved.

Prayer

Dear God, thank you for your abundant grace. Thank you for carrying me in the good times and in the hard times. I admit that without you, I can do nothing. But in you, I can do anything and everything you call me to do. Thank you for being a perfect parent to me and to my children. In Jesus' Name, Amen.

TWENTY-SIX

The Power in God's Promises

Cheri Fuller

I keep asking that the God of our Lord Jesus Christ, the glorious
Father, may give you the Spirit of wisdom and revelation, so that you may
know him better. I pray that the eyes of your heart may be enlightened in
order that you may know the hope to which he has called you, the riches of
his glorious inheritance in his holy people, and his incomparably great
power for us who believe.

Ephesians 1:17-19 (NIV)

I love the verse that says, "God is the one who keeps every promise forever" (Psalm 146:66), a truth that is echoes throughout Scripture. His Book, the Bible, contains thousands of promises, such as "Nothing can separate you from my love," in Romans 8:38-39. Or the great assurance of "Draw near to me and I will draw near to you" in James 4:8.

As a thirty-year-old, I was drawn to prayer in part because circumstance like our son's frequent ER visits for a chronic illness had made me aware that I was not in control.

I was also broken-hearted about my big sister's struggling with addiction, and my mother was diagnosed with an advanced stage of cancer and died 4 ½ months later. When difficult times came, my concerns propelled me to turn to God and his promises.

Over the years I discovered and practiced different ways to pray: to take prayer walks in our neighborhood, to lead women in Moms in Prayer groups, to pray God's word, and to persevere—PUSH, or Pray Until Something Happens and not give up.

You see, as I read the Bible day by day, I was storing God's promises in my heart and they fueled my prayers. For example, a particular prayer in Ephesians 1:17-19 for our sons: "I keep asking that God will give them the Spirit of wisdom and revelation so that they may know God better. I pray that the eyes of my sons' hearts will be enlightened so they will know the hope they're called to ... and God's incomparably great power for us who believe."

When the oldest started high school, my husband and I looked at each other one night and said, "Nothing prepared us for this, did it?" He turned from God, church and youth group into all things involving parties, girlfriends, and whatever the world had to offer.

Yet I continued asking God to open the eyes of his heart and give him a spirit of wisdom so he might know God better.

Nothing changed for six long years.

In college he wasn't in a Bible study or seeming to move toward God. When he came home one weekend, after Sunday morning breakfast I asked, "Are you going to church with us, honey?" He answered that it was his faith and he needed to deal with it himself.

Time passed but the promise shined brightly, propelling my prayers.

The outcome of this long-range prayer occurred at the end of his sophomore year of college. After finals in May, he moved back home but had no prospects for a summer job. Following dinner that night, he asked me to drive him across the city to I-35 so he could have his overheated car towed. On the way, he talked about how his relationship with his girlfriend had gone sour and how stressed out he was.

Then he turned and said, "Mom, I've been feeling so empty and lonely, living so far from God and trying to do everything on my own. I know that God hasn't moved. I have. And more than anything I want to have an intimate relationship with Christ."

My heart leaped with so much joy I could have jumped out of the car. I didn't, because I was driving.

Our son's life took a 180 turn toward Christ from that moment on. He grew in his faith over the months and year and never looked back. Today he's a dedicated father and husband, and a committed believer who is impacting the lives of others.

When we pray God's promises, we are laying down the circuits for God's unlimited power to come in our life and the lives of those we love and pray for. Prayer is a catalyst to bring forth what God has promised. It's our greatest resource for hearts to be changed and spiritual eyes to be opened.

Who came to your mind as you read this story—a husband, an adult daughter, a troubled friend? Pray these verses in Ephesians 1:17-19 and put his or her name into it. Don't just pray it today but persevere until the answer comes. And know that God hears and in his timing, he will answer!

Prayer

Dearest God, thank you for your promise that you are always with me. Thank you for being faithful even when my faith fails. As I serve you as a mother to the ones you've entrusted to my care and nurture, help me to do so out of the overflow of the love I receive from you so that in seasons of waiting – and not seeing – I can still declare, "I believe!" In Jesus' Name, Amen.

TWENTY-SEVEN

How to Find a Happy Ending

Christie Purifoy

My heart overflows with a pleasing theme.

Psalm 45:1 (ESV)

M y daughter, my firstborn, slips through the kitchen door. I don't know if I should blame the summer humidity or another night of troubled sleep, but her long hair looks like a creature from a nightmare world.

"I had another bad dream last night. A dream about me and baby Elsa," she says.

"What happened?" her younger brother asks.

Half listening, I run the rubber spatula through the eggs. Lily says something about witches and a chase.

"That's when I woke up, so I imagined a happy ending to make myself feel better."

"Oh?" I say. "What happy ending?"

81

"Elsa and I found a beautiful castle and a prince. We ran into the castle and turned into princesses, and we were safe. It was the only thing I could think of."

These last words are spoken on a downward mumble. When I turn around she doesn't meet my eye, as if she knows what I am thinking: *You are almost ten. Haven't you outgrown these sentimental royal kingdom fantasies?*

A few weeks after we moved to this Victorian red-brick farmhouse, my husband built a small tree house in the shape of a castle. I had written a to-do list with a thousand more important tasks. Set up a dehumidifier in the old dirt basement. Exchange our Florida license plate for Pennsylvania. Figure out how to keep the cranky clothes dryer from stalling mid-cycle. When I saw the flag flying from the castle's corner turret, all was forgiven. License plates may be the law, but a royal lion stenciled in blue spray-paint is magic.

If our daughter's idea of a happy ending is limited to castles and princes, we have only ourselves to blame. While my husband realizes medieval fantasies in treated pine, I read fairytales and buy royal robes for the costume box. I remember a cone-shaped princess hat particularly well. The veil is tattered and the pink silk is stained, but I felt conflicted when I found it crushed beneath a pile of Jedi Knight accessories. I can't remember the last time I saw it frame my daughter's face. I suppose she traded it for a neon t-shirt decorated with peace signs. It is a transition I find both right and, somehow, incredibly sad.

While the morning's scrambled eggs harden on six different plates, I read my Bible. I do not choose Psalm 45, but it has been chosen for me. At first, I smile in surprise. How appropriate, I think. After reading, I am ashamed. How dare I despise my daughter's fantasy?

The Psalmist sings, *'My heart overflows with a pleasing theme."* His vision of a King and bride is neither sentimental nor is it childish. It is simply beautiful. This is an ancient wedding song, but it speaks of a wedding we have yet to see. It is the past and future of my daughter's dream. It reveals the roots of her desire and the promise of its fulfillment.

The earthly kings of history and fairytale are only shadows of this perfect, righteous Lord. Princesses in their pearls and pointy hats are pale imitations of his bride, the Church. This King who rides for truth and righteousness is the embodiment of my daughter's midnight dream.

I had thought it right that the pink silk hat be discarded. I consoled myself over the torn veil by assuming we all, mother and daughter, husband and sons, must leave this fantasy behind. I was wrong. A costume or a castle is not necessarily a toy to be neglected. It might be a portal. It might be a path. Heading deeper within, we find the fulfillment of a God-given desire. We find the solid realness of what had been a shimmery dream. Even better, we discover that every nightmare has been defeated.

My two sons fight imaginary dragons with plywood shields, but they enact a battle that has already been won. The arrows and sword of the Psalmist's vision were real, but they took the unexpected form of a cross. The "mighty one" of Psalm 45 achieved victory by shedding his own blood. And he did it beneath a sign that said King.

I close my Bible. I stand up. I see my daughter through the kitchen window. Her wild hair is dangling over the castle's edge, and she is shouting something to her brothers below. I want to go to her. To all of them. I want to say I know the name of the prince she found in her dream. His name is Jesus. He is Christ our King.

Prayer

Dear Heavenly Father, thank you for how you remind me of grace and truth as I go about my everyday life – through your word, through my children, and even through my own story. May my children see you doing the same in their lives and may they be drawn to you continually as you pursue their hearts as you redeem nightmares with your love and grace. In Jesus' Name, Amen.

TWENTY-EIGHT

God's Promise for the Daily Life of a Mom

Sue Detweiler

But now, this is what the LORD says—he who created you, Jacob, he who formed you, Israel: "Do not fear, for I have redeemed you; I have summoned you by name; you are mine."

Isaiah 43:1 (NIV)

H oping that God's promise would be real in my daily life, I was in a battle.

Every mom that I know desires to be the best mom in world, but often she feels like the worst.

I remember one of my worst "mom-moments." I was driving to a Saturday night worship service rehearsing in my mind the way that I had just lost my temper with my daughter.

My knuckles were white as I gripped the steering wheel. Tears streamed down my face and were reflected in the eyes of my two toddlers strapped in their car seats. Another baby girl was growing inside my belly, tucked in tight under my seatbelt.

Just hours before, my irritation had taken a sharp turn into exasperation when my daughter spilled grape juice on my newly mopped floor. Feeling overwhelmed, trapped, and exhausted, I just wanted to take a nap.

I knew I needed to get out of the house. My husband was working an extra job to help make ends meet. I was alone in the kitchen. Even though we were pastors at a local church, on Saturday nights I liked to load the girls up and visit someone else's church where I could just sit in the pews and receive.

Now, the negative thoughts continued in my brain . . . "What am I thinking? Me, trying to be a mother . . . God, ARE YOU THERE?"

The last question seemed to bounce off the soiled ceiling of my car. Somehow I maneuvered into a parking space. Carrying the car seat in one hand and squeezing too tightly the fingers of my oldest daughter with the other hand, I walked into church as a defeated mother. After signing them into childcare, I breathed a sigh of relief.

I don't think I heard the sermon that night. I just remembered communion. As my screaming tirades flashed back in my mind, I began to sob. My hands shook as I held a communion cup. The fight intensified in my mind.

"Who do you think you are? You hypocrite . . . You will never change . . ."

This last thought was interrupted by the pastor speaking from the pulpit: "I believe there are some of you who have believed a lie that you can't change. The truth is that Jesus' blood has paid the price for your sin, and He has delivered you out of darkness. You are free. You just need to believe it, receive it, and then act on it."

It sounded so simple. Why was I so bound? The turmoil within me began to bubble up, then calm, as though the toxic thoughts had finally been neutralized by the truth of God's Word.

A new phrase began to take shape in my mind. It was an entirely different thought. It felt like a whisper from heaven that I was finally listening to. "You are the best mom in the world for your children . . . I have called you . . . I will help you be a better mom . . . You can trust Me."

Hope began to fill the deepest recesses of my soul. For so long I had floundered under the fog of the enemy's torment. These words were like beams of sunshine, bringing a multifaceted rainbow of His promise: His personal promise to me. That night, as I took communion in faith, my life began to change.

Prayer

Dear Heavenly Father, thank you for meeting me at my point of need— always. Thank you for calling me to be the mother of my children. Thank you for equipping me moment-by-moment to be the one to lead these young hearts and minds to you—the only perfect Parent. In Jesus' Name, Amen.

TWENTY-NINE

No Fear!

Stephanie Shott

For God has not given us a spirit of fear, but of power and of love and of a sound mind.

2 Timothy 1:7 (NKJV)

C hildren are often afraid of things that aren't real, things that could never happen and things that don't make sense.

Some of their fears are irrational—others are not. But whatever the basis of the fears that haunt their little hearts, you can help them overcome their fears by the way you act and react to the things they are afraid of.

Some of the fears they have are fears that you have. It's easy to transfer those fears from your heart to theirs by the way you respond to things. Unfortunately, fear can be debilitating and can rob you and your children of your God-given destinies. But there is a way to overcome fear for you and your children. It's called faith.

- *Faith in a God who is bigger than any fear you or your children have.*

- *Faith that is strengthened when you spend time in the Word of God.*

- *Faith that is demonstrated when you believe what He says.*

- *Faith that moves mountains and opens doors when it ascends from the heart of a believer to the heart of God through a simple thing called prayer.*

Today, I want to encourage you to pray 2 Timothy 1:7 for your children—and if you have any irrational fears, pray that same verse for yourself, as well. Remember . . . when you fear God, you have nothing else to fear!

Prayer

Dear God, You have not given us a spirit of fear, but of power and of love and of a sound mind. Help me to remember this and give me the wisdom to teach this to my children. May our trust in your always win out over any fear that tries to hinder us. In Jesus' Name, Amen.

THIRTY

Walking Blindly, Trusting Completely

Shelley Hendrix and Brianne Rask

When the Holy Spirit, who is truth, comes, he shall guide you into all truth, for he will not be presenting his own ideas, but will be passing on to you what he has heard.

John 16:13a (NLT)

My sister, Brianne, texted me to share this sweet story with me and gave me permission to share it with you:

I had to take Mattie (twelve-year-old daughter) for a homeschool test today. When we got there, she helped get Phoebe (three and a half years old) out of the car. There was a really sweet exchange between them:

Phoebe had sun in her eyes. She walked a few steps toward the street. Eyes closed. With her hand in the air. Trusting that her big sister would grab that little hand and guide her across the street. And sure enough, her big sister came through and got her safely across the parking lot.

God spoke to me in that moment, I really feel like He did. That's how we should trust Him. We can blindly walk into what may seem to be danger, with our hands to heaven, knowing He will take our hand and guide us through it.

This made me think of the promise Jesus left His followers (including us) when He said that the Holy Spirit would be our guide (John 16:13). We don't have to go it alone - in fact, we can't even if we want to! Our God is always with us. *But our experience with Him will be determined by our trust in Him.*

Prayer

Father, I pray that we will choose, like sweet little Phoebe, to raise our hand—even if our eyes are closed to what's ahead—and trust that YOU, our Heavenly Father, walk beside us and that Your Spirit within us will guide us. In Jesus' Name, Amen.

THIRTY-ONE

Raising a Jonah

Michelle LaRowe

"Go to the great city of Nineveh and preach against it, because its wickedness has come up before me." But Jonah ran away from the Lord and headed for Tarshish. He went down to Joppa, where he found a ship bound for that port. After paying the fare, he went aboard and sailed for Tarshish to flee from the Lord.

Jonah 1:2-3 (NIV)

D*isobedient.*
Ignorant.
Judgmental.
Stubborn.
Dramatic.
Negative.
Argumentative.

While the adjectives above may read like a checklist describing a typical teenager who's having a bad day, they're actually words that describe one of the Bible's better-known characters. While he's best known for ending up in the belly of a giant fish, Jonah has a lot more in common with today's teenagers than you may think.

It's no secret that the teenage years are filled with parenting challenges, most often revolving around self-discovery—the sorting out of convictions, the bucking of authority and the development of independent opinions (which often radically differ from the folks'). These struggles are enough to make some parents wish they could escape into a fish's belly themselves.

But Christian parents can take heart. In one small book (consisting of just four short chapters), parents of teenagers can learn big lessons to help them successfully ride the waves of the teenage years.

Jonah's story

"'Go to the great city of Nineveh and preach against it, because its wickedness has come up before me.' But Jonah ran away from the Lord and headed for Tarshish. He went down to Joppa, where he found a ship bound for that port. After paying the fare, he went aboard and sailed for Tarshish to flee from the Lord" (Jonah 1:2-3).

Jonah's story starts out quite simply. God gave Jonah a specific and straightforward command. And what did Jonah do?

He ran.

He hid.

He was disobedient.

But God wasn't going to let him off that easy.

"Then the Lord sent a great wind on the sea, and such a violent storm arose that the ship threatened to break up" (1:4).

So Jonah went into the bottom of the ship and fell asleep, ignoring the situation at hand, acting as if nothing was happening. Jonah was so ignorant that he didn't even see how his actions were affecting others. When his shipmates (who soon discovered that Jonah was running from God) confronted him, he told them to pick him up and throw him into the sea, knowing that if this happened the raging storm would calm.

God sent a fish that swallowed Jonah, and Jonah stayed in the belly of the fish for three days and three nights. But inside the fish, in the depth and darkness of the ocean, Jonah repented and prayed to God for his deliverance. And God heard him and answered him, commanding the fish to spit Jonah out.

God gave Jonah another chance, commanding him again to *"go to the great city of Nineveh and proclaim to it the message I give you"* (3:2). So Jonah went and announced to the Ninevites, *'Forty more days and Nineveh will be overturned"* (3:4). The Ninevites believed the message and cleaned up their act.

"When God saw what they did and how they turned from their evil ways, he had compassion and did not bring upon them the destruction he had threatened" (3:10).

Perhaps you're surprised to discover the Ninevites' repentance made Jonah angry. He had delivered God's message, but the outcome wasn't what he thought it should have been. Much of the rest of the Book of Jonah demonstrates the prophet's lack of compassion as he argues with God about God's mercy toward the city.

Raising your 'Jonah'

While the people and places may be different in this ancient biblical narrative than in your home, the struggles, attitudes and characteristics of Jonah may be a bit too familiar. In fact, if you replace Jonah's name with your teenager's, you may be surprised at just how close to home this story hits. But if we look closely at the story, we see that God understood Jonah, his struggles and his emotions, and we can use God's methods of "parenting" Jonah to parent our own teen during challenging times.

The next time your teen throws a pity party, turns into a drama queen or runs from what you (or God!) has asked them to do, put God's parenting methods to the test.

1. Give God the chance to bring things to light.

As parents, we are right in wanting to know what's going on with our teens. But sometimes we push so hard to find out information, we don't allow God to make the unknown known. Just as God exposed Jonah's sin, He has ways of revealing sin issues in your child's life if you ask Him.

2. Hold your teen accountable.

God didn't let Jonah just run away. Jonah had to answer for what he had done. Establish a system of accountability with your teen. If you notice she's heading down the wrong track, gently confront her and help her get back on track (see Galatians 6:1-2).

3. Remember that although your teen may run from his circumstances, he can't run from God's presence (Psalm 139:7-8).

Jonah was in the belly of a fish, and God was still with him. Trust that God is with your teen, even in the moments when your teen turns away from God. Remember, sometimes your child will have to be in the depth of darkness to really call out.

4. God still paid attention to Jonah's needs, even though he was being difficult.

When your teen acts like he doesn't need you or want your help, be a presence and meet his needs.

5. Be a parent of second chances.

Just as God gave Jonah a second chance to be obedient, do the same for your teen.

6. Don't be moved by your teen's drama.

God's actions weren't contingent on Jonah's response. Your parenting decisions must be made on what you feel is best for your teen.

7. Raise your teen to respond to the Holy Spirit's conviction.

Don't overuse parental condemnation. With Jonah, it took God's dramatic conviction of sin to bring about right behavior. The Holy Spirit can bring your teen back to God and back to doing what is right.

8. When things get tough, trust God to get through!

God will never stop trying to get your teen's attention. As with Jonah, God knows what it takes to get through to your teen. God is there, even in the moments of drama and self-pity.

9. Don't pass up teachable moments.

Even when your teen seems unreceptive, clearly communicate godly expectations. God continued to teach Jonah about compassion, even when the prophet seemed unreceptive.

10. Ask questions.

Sometimes all it takes is a rhetorical question to help your teen see things in a different light. The Book of Jonah ends with God's question to the prophet.

Jonah's story doesn't wrap itself up neatly. You and your teen will face some challenging times and unresolved issues. But if God could take a rebellious prophet and guide him, He can do the same for your child. You can trust Him to bring about the best in your teen's life.

Prayer

Dear God, some days are much harder than others in this parenting journey. I pray for the wisdom to parent well and the courage to make hard choices along the way. Thank you for the hope I can hang onto in realizing that there is never a moment of time that my child is outside of your view or care. In Jesus' Name, Amen.

THIRTY-TWO

"You Were a Good Mama Today"

Monica Gil

My son, do not despise the LORD's discipline and do not resent his rebuke, because the LORD disciplines those he loves, as a father the son he delights in.

Proverbs 3:11-12 (NIV)

It was one of those days. A day of tantrums and testing. Grace was in an utter state of rebellion. I liken the battle to subvert the sin in her heart to that of the 101st Airborne on the eve of defending Bastogne in World War II. General McCollough's orders were clear: "You do what you have to do—but you hold this line."

"Hold the line!" These are the words I say to myself when we enter the battleground of rebellion. These are the words I say to Doug and to every parent I see in exasperation as they fight to train up and civilize their children. "Hold the Line!" If we imagine this is anything less than warfare—real spiritual warfare, we are fooling ourselves!

When the exhaustion of the day came to a close I tucked Gracie—age 3—in bed. While it was a tough day of battle, our love was not

98

diminished. As we snuggled she gently pressed her hand to my cheek and whispered: "You were a good Mama today."

Wow. The depth of that statement plunged into my heart. This was more than an affirmation from my child for good discipline. This was more than affirmation from the Lord encouraging me as a parent. I realized this was a deep spiritual truth about our relationship with The Lord. When we face His rebuke in the spiritual warfare against our own sin—how do we react?

My son, do not despise the LORD's discipline and do not resent his rebuke, because the LORD disciplines those he loves, as a father the son he delights in (Proverbs 3:11-12).

This is a tough truth. How often do I find myself either in rebellion or despair over the Lord's rebuke? More often than I care to admit. But the truth is, as we move deeper into relationship with our Father, He does more to reveal our besetting sins and our unhealthy idols. He "disciplines" us toward His righteousness.

Look at Hebrews from The Message translation: (my emphasis)

So don't feel sorry for yourselves. Or have you forgotten how good parents treat children, and that God regards you as his children? My dear child, don't shrug off God's discipline, but don't be crushed by it either. It's the child he loves that he disciplines; the child he embraces, he also corrects.... Only irresponsible parents leave children to fend for themselves. Would you prefer an irresponsible God? We respect our own parents for training and not spoiling us, so why not embrace God's training so we can truly live? While we were children, our parents did what seemed best to them. But God is doing what is best for us ... At the time, discipline isn't much fun ... Later, of course, it pays off handsomely, for it's the well-trained who find themselves mature in their relationship with God.

It's that last piece I love best—finding ourselves "mature" in our relationship with God.

Are we growing up in the Lord? Do we let Him in, allow Him access to our hearts to admonish us, discipline and refine us, train us in His righteousness and crush the idols of our hearts? After a rough day of enduring His discipline do we have the undiminished love and courage to crawl into The Father's arms and say . . .

"Abba, Father—You were a good Daddy today."

Those whom I love I rebuke and discipline. So be earnest, and repent. Here I am! I stand at the door and knock . . . (Revelation 3:19-20)(NIV).

Prayer

Dear Abba Father, indeed you are a good daddy today and always. Thank you for loving me, your child, well enough to discipline when necessary. Help me to remember how loved I am by you in those moments. May the same be true as we parent our child(ren). May they know how loved they are always. In Jesus' Name, Amen.

THIRTY-THREE

God Interrupted

Alison Everill

My help comes from the Lord,
the Maker of heaven and earth.
He will not let your foot slip—
he who watches over you will not slumber;
indeed, he who watches over Israel
will neither slumber nor sleep.

Psalm 121:2-4 (NIV)

I am not a good sleeper. My mind goes so fast all the time that I have a hard time shutting it down when it's time to crawl in bed and call it a day. So, an uninterrupted night of sleep for me is a rare commodity. A couple of weeks ago, my active mind was just losing the fight with my over-extended body and I was drifting off to that wonderful world of REM. It was about 1:30 in the morning and just as I was closing my eyes I heard, "Mommy, I need you."

My youngest son was leaning on the banister of the stairs with his tattered blanket slung over his shoulder asking for my help. What was I going to do? Ignore him? Get angry and think, "How dare he interrupt my sleep! Doesn't he know that I need to rest?" No. Even though I was bone tired, the love of motherhood would not allow me to ignore him. He needed me and I was there.

As I helped him get settled back in for the night I lay beside him for just a moment and kissed his perfect cheek. Even though he was asleep almost immediately and probably didn't hear me, I whispered to him of my love for him and Jesus' love for him. I told him that he could call me anytime day or night and I would come running.

As I left him to his sleep and went back downstairs to finish the night, I thought about how what I had just experienced was a smaller scale of the Father's reaction to me when I call upon Him. It doesn't matter to Him when I call, He is always available. And what's even more incredible is that, unlike earthly parents, He never slumbers or sleeps (Psalm 121). He relentlessly watches over me and even longs to hear from me.

Scripture is filled with requests from our wonderful Father to come to him and talk to him and even ask for what we need. Why don't we do this? Is it because we think that He doesn't have time, or that He doesn't really care – that our requests are too small for such a big God? If we let that train of thought dominate our prayer life, we will never have the intimacy with Christ that He died to provide. Remember, He did die for you and it was not only to make a way for you to get to heaven, it was also to make a way for you to have fellowship with the Father. It must grieve His heart when we don't take advantage of the privileges He died to give us.

What's the point? We are God's children and He loves us. He wants to be "interrupted" by our requests even if it is the middle of the night. The veil of the temple was torn in two. He was trying to say something when He did that (Hebrews 4:12). So call on Him.

Prayer

Dear Heavenly Father, what a privilege it is – beyond description, in fact—that I can come to you at any time; and that when I do so, I am always doing so at Your invitation. "Thank you" seems so inadequate, but I am absolutely grateful. May I pass this invitation on to my children so that they, too, can know where their help comes from and how delighted you are when they enter into your presence. In Jesus' Name, Amen.

THIRTY-FOUR

Water Closet Praying

Dena Dyer

I call on you, O God, for you will answer me; give ear to me and hear my prayer.

Psalm 17:6 (NIV)

Do you constantly feel guilty about not praying or reading the Bible enough—if at all?

I used to feel that way. As a busy mom of crazy boys, when the dishwasher broke, my hormones raged, a work deadline loomed, and the kids whined, sometimes I just wanted to scream.

And fit in a daily quiet time? You've got to be kidding me!

That's why Susanna Wesley, one of the mothers of the Methodist church, has always been one of my role models. In addition to being an Anglican minister's wife, Susanna managed a full-to-the-rim household, homeschooled her children (even writing some of their textbooks), and studied theology. When her husband was away, she filled his pulpit.

Eventually her fifteenth child, John, and her seventeenth, Charles, founded the Methodist church. Whew. The overview of her life makes me tired just writing it! Yet Susanna's most admirable trait? She was never too busy for spiritual nourishment.

John Wesley once recorded that his mother never let anything interfere with her times with God. Often, she would put her apron over to head to signal that she was not to be disturbed during prayer time. I don't have an apron. (As one writer friend of mine says, "My apron burned in the fire.") But I did come up with a way to be alone and pray, even during the hair-raising, raising-toddler years.

As a busy mom who needed and wanted to pray, I asked God for ways to find peace in my prayer life, instead of always feeling guilty. I felt frustrated and scatterbrained—I could rarely remember whom or what I had promised to pray for.

So one day when I had a few hours by myself, I wrote down every need (for myself, family, friends, church, community, nation, and world) I could think of. Then I divided them into thirty-one equal segments and put them in a notebook. I placed this notebook—believe it or not—in the bathroom, where I had a few precious minutes alone each day. (This also fulfills Jesus' command to "go into your closet and pray," though I'm not sure He actually meant a water closet!) As author Anne Lamott once said, "Some people think God is in the details. But I have come to believe God is in the bathroom."

In my closet, I spoke to God about the items that corresponded to the day of the month. That way, I could pray over the multitude of needs in my life—one day and one minute at a time. My kids are older now, and I pray in different ways, but I have fond memories of calling out to God and receiving peace while toddler fingers curled up around the bottom of the door and voices cried, "Mommy, when are you done?" (It's really true—the days are long but the years are short.)

Maybe you need to find a creative way to spend time with God. If "water closet praying" isn't for you, here are some different ideas about fitting prayer into a full schedule:

Pray as you work out.

Light a candle when someone dear to you has a need. Every time you see the flame, lift her or his request up to God.

Pray while driving/commuting.

Pray while waiting on kids at sports practices.

Sign up for prayer lists online, and pray as you read the e-mail messages.

And remember, no matter how or when we choose to pray, God is pleased when we make the effort. He just wants to hear from us— even if our calls come from the bathroom!

Prayer

Heavenly Father, thank you for the reminder that I am important to you; and that you want to spend time with me. May I not view a "quiet time" as another item to check off an already overwhelmed to-do list, but as an invitation to come and be fully me engaged with you in the present. Thank you for the freedom to speak to you at any time and in any place—even the bathroom! In Jesus' Name, Amen.

This is excerpted and edited from Dena's book, Grace for the Race: Meditations for Busy Moms *(Barbour 2004).*

THIRTY-FIVE

Keep Her Safe, Lord

Jan Dunlap

You will keep in perfect peace those whose minds are steadfast, because they trust in you.

Isaiah 26:3 (NIV)

"Mom," my oldest daughter said on the phone on Monday, "I wanted to let you and Dad know that I'm heading to Africa tonight with my team. We'll be in Liberia, Senegal, Guinea, and Sierra Leone, then back to D.C. by the end of the week."

I'd been anticipating the call for days, since my daughter works for the United States Agency for International Development and has been involved in the agency's efforts to coordinate international response to the spread of the Ebola virus. After our brief conversation, I realized that my own initial reaction of fear and concern must be similar to the one shared by every parent whose child is called into a potentially dangerous situation by virtue of career choice.

My second reaction was to remind myself that my daughter is in God's hands, and no amount of worrying on my part will change His plans for her, no matter what those plans may be. Of course, that is much easier said than done, isn't it? What mother doesn't worry about her children, even her grown ones?

Over the years of raising my own brood, I've often thought that the most difficult time to 'put my money where my mouth is' spiritually has been when I have to trust God with my children's welfare. Not that I've always done such a stellar job of it, myself, mind you. (Exhibit #1: I will never forget the day my energetic three-year-old son went bounding out the back door, only to have the glass door he didn't realize was there shatter around him. He looked bewildered on the other side of the splintered door, and I was almost in shock to see what he had done, but as soon as I scooped him up outside and found him totally uninjured—not even a tiny cut!—I thanked God for assigning such an alert guardian angel to my wild boy. I was humbled by God's provision . . . and I vowed to never have a glass door again.)

The truth, of which I remind myself daily, is that God, not me, is in charge of what happens to my kids. If I truly believe God's promises of His eternal care, then it's my own shortcoming when I fear for my children.

Matthew 7:9 pops into my head: *"Which of you, if your son asks for bread, will give him a stone?"* Of course, we'll give our son the bread he asks for, and we know that our Father in heaven will go us at least one—if not a thousand!—better. That is who God is—generous in love.

Our job as parents, then, is to believe God so completely that we know our children are in good hands always, because those hands belong to God.

"You will keep in perfect peace those whose minds are steadfast, because they trust in you" (Isaiah 26:3).

That's the kind of peace every parent can use, wouldn't you say? Lord, make it so.

Prayer

Indeed, Lord, make it so. Help me to trust in You, ultimately, for the care of my children. Keep my heart and mind at peace as I entrust my own brood to a faithful Father. In Jesus' Name, Amen.

THIRTY-SIX

Grace Thoughts (on Aging)

Karen Jordan

Teach us to number our days, that we may gain a heart of wisdom.

Psalm 90:12 (NIV)

I can't believe my daughter Tara turned 39 this past week! And I don't want to be ashamed to admit it.

Why are women so concerned and sensitive about their age?

I remember when I couldn't wait to turn 18—then 21. The next year, my dad died of pancreatic cancer at the age of 47—the same disease that his mother died of in her early sixties.

So, after Dad's death, my view of life changed. What if I died young of some horrible disease like my dad?

Dreading birthdays

By the time I turned 29, I stopped celebrating my birthdays because I dreaded turning a year older. Oh, my family remembered every one of them with presents and some sort of party. But the threat of aging hung overhead like a heavy dark cloud.

A few of my closest friends and relatives even noticed my insecurities about aging. In fact, since our birthdays were only a few days apart, my younger cousin, Gary, joked a lot with me about "getting old," until a few years after I turned 40.

Grieving a loss

I grieved when Gary lost his battle to pancreatic cancer at the young age of 35. He never celebrated his fortieth birthday. He missed watching his three beautiful daughters grow up. And he never met his precious grandchildren. He didn't even live long enough to grow old with the wife of his youth.

Gary did share his faith stories with me the last time I visited with him—he found his peace with God as he faced death. And after his death, my view of "getting old" changed.

Not long after Gary's death, we also lost my two-year-old nephew, my mother, my uncle (Gary's dad), and several other close friends and family. And these unexpected tragedies forced me to deal with my own mortality, advancing with each year's new health challenges.

Celebrating life

Now, I want to celebrate "getting old," not dread it!

But I still struggle with my emotions as I address that old habit of worry. Every day, I must consider God's Truth about growing older. I can't see the truth through the eyes of today's culture.

With "Grace Talk" we can confess this truth to our souls, "Teach us to number our days, that we may gain a heart of wisdom" (Psalm 90:12 NIV).

Believing God's Promises

I hope you will also consider this promise from God's Word: "Now God has us where he wants us, with all the time in this world and the next to shower grace and kindness upon us . . ." (Ephesians 2:8-10 MSG).

Prayer

Lord, forgive me for not embracing and enjoying every season of my life. Thank You for the gift of a long life, so I can enjoy my marriage, my children, and grandchildren. And Lord, whatever time I have left on Your awesome planet, please help me to live it with gratitude, acknowledging the gift and power grace in my life. Amen.

THIRTY-SEVEN

He Thinks I am Wonderful

Shelley Hendrix

I praise You because I am fearfully and wonderfully made; Your works are wonderful, I know that full well.

Psalm 139:14 (NIV)

The day he was born, I looked deep into his beautiful eyes and said, "I think you are wonnnn . . . derrrrr . . . ful."

And I did.

I still do.

Even though I haven't always experienced "wonderfulness" from him. Some days are just plain harder than others, aren't they?

In those hard times, I try to remind myself of things like this:

Through his baby, toddler, and preschool years, this kid wanted to marry *me*, y'all. (I'm smiling as I remember that over-the-top adorableness of time already gone by too soon.)

Little girls would find themselves smitten by my son (but of course!), whom I've nicknamed my Boy Wonder (ever since that first of many times I've said, "I think you are wonderful!"); and he never seemed to reciprocate any of their crushes. He would simply tell them, "I'm going to marry my mommy."

Of course those years and that sentiment couldn't last forever. He is no longer that tiny blonde-headed Prince Charming that told me how beautiful I look when I wear necklaces and bracelets. He's healthy enough emotionally to no longer want to marry me.

But, you know what? Even now, as a middle schooler with all the wacky realities of being an adolescent boy, that boy-becoming-a-man still thinks that I am wonderful—*most* of the time.

When I was expecting my son, Boy Mamas told me, "Nothing prepares you for a boy. You're going to be loved like you've never been loved before."

So, mamas, whether you're a "boy mama," a "girl mama," or, like me, have both genders under your wing, as you raise those crazy, unpredictable mini-humans on days that make you want to pull your hair out—grab a photo of that bright-eyed boy or girl that stole your heart and remind yourself of the times that make mothering worthwhile, and whisper once again, "I think that (s)he is wonderful!"

Prayer

Dear Heavenly Father, I think you are wonderful! Thank you for thinking the same of me—and of my children. May we love well as we have been so well loved. In Jesus' Name, Amen.

THIRTY-EIGHT

Having God's "More Than Enough"

Cindi McMenamin

You have filled my heart with greater joy than when their grain and new wine abound. I will lie down and sleep in peace, for you alone, O Lord, make me dwell in safety.

Psalm 4:7-8 (ESV)

I remember the day we were driving home from a store, and my teenage daughter was complaining to me about all the things her friends had that she didn't – new cars driven by her sixteen-year-old friends who just got their driver's licenses, expansive homes with more rooms than their families needed, the latest electronic gadgets, the fanciest clothes, the highest-priced handbags.

Weary of constantly being reminded of what we didn't have that her friends' families did, I finally blew! "Do you realize what we do have?" I snapped. "You have a roof over your head and these days, that should be enough!"

I didn't know I had just struck a chord with her. Her face fell and she sadly told me of another one of her friends who was losing her home due to debt and a parent's job loss. Immediately my tone softened as I realized my daughter had already been convicted by her own words. We prayed for the family that was losing their home, and then I silently prayed for wisdom to turn that topic into a teaching moment.

"You know, Sweetie," I told her softly, as I continued to drive, "a lot of people around us are losing their homes. That's why it's important for us to not only think about what we have and be grateful for it, but to focus on what we have that we will never lose." She looked at me for a moment. And then she got it.

We immediately began to recount all that we have that can never be taken from us:

- The love we have from each other in our family
- The memories we've had in our three-bedroom condo (and the small house we owned before we moved to a more expensive area of California)
- The unconditional love of God (Romans 5:8)
- The gift of our salvation (Ephesians 2:8-9)
- A promised mansion in Eternity (John 14:2-3)

I realized that day that my daughter is not the only one who often wishes she had more. It's easy for me, at times, to look at what others have and be envious. It's natural for me to sometimes wish I had a little more extra money to indulge in my desires. But so often I forget all I do have . . . and that it is *more than enough.*

I came across some convicting statistics recently that convinced me of this: If you have food in your refrigerator, clothes on your back,

a roof overhead, and a place to sleep, you are richer than 75 percent of the people in this world! If you have any money in the bank and some in your wallet, and some spare change in a dish somewhere, you are among the top 8 percent of the world's wealthy; 92 percent have less to live on than you do! If you have never experienced the danger of battle, the loneliness of imprisonment, the agony of torture or the pangs of starvation, you are ahead of 500 million other people in the world. If you can attend worship services at church without the fear of harassment, arrest, torture or death, you are more blessed than three billion people in the world.[1]

So often we go through life looking at what others have and wondering when our ship will come in. Then we remember we have a God who owns the cattle on a thousand hills (Psalm 50:10), a God who has gone to prepare a place for us and who will come again and receive us to Himself so that where He is, we will be—forever (John 14:3).

In Psalm 4, David the Psalmist was asking God for relief from his distresses. But then he must have remembered what he had, because he finished his prayer with a song of perspective and joy: "You have filled my heart with greater joy than when their grain and new wine abound. I will lie down and sleep in peace, for you alone, O Lord, make me dwell in safety" (vv 7-8). In another translation, that verse sounds like a song I should be singing every day that I begin to forget my blessings and long for more: "I have God's more-than-enough, more joy in one ordinary day than they get in all their shopping sprees. At days' end I'm ready for sound sleep. For you, God, have put my life back together" (MSG).

God is the true source of security in an insecure world . . . and He is the Only One who satisfies in a world where we can never get

---

[1] Statistics taken from Warren, Kay, *Dangerous Surrender* (New York: Zondervan, 2007).

enough. And when we have Him—along with His promises for provision, protection and peace—we have "more than enough."

Can you draw strength from knowing that you have God's more-than-enough even if at times it doesn't look like quite enough? Thank Him today for all that you have, as well as for the blessings that you don't yet see. The Bible says if we belong to Christ, God has blessed us in the heavenly realm with every spiritual blessing in Christ (Ephesians 1:3). And if we "share in His sufferings" we are "heirs or God and co-heirs with Christ" (Romans 8:17). Joint heirs with God! Think about that. We are heirs of all that is His. Now that's an inheritance. That's a future. That is more than enough.

Do you realize you have the capacity to have more joy in one ordinary day than the rest of the world has in all their shopping sprees? Then live in that freedom . . . and help your children rejoice in it!

Prayer

Dear Father, I admit that in you and because of you, I have more than enough! Thank you for taking such good care of me and my family. May I become increasingly grateful and may I pass along that attribute and attitude to my children. In Jesus' Name, Amen.

THIRTY-NINE

U R Enough (Even When It Doesn't Feel Like It)

Jennifer Strickland

No, in all these things we are more than conquerors through him who loved us. For I am convinced that neither death nor life, neither angels nor demons, neither the present nor the future, nor any powers, neither height nor depth, nor anything else in all creation, will be able to separate us from the love of God that is in Christ Jesus our Lord.

Romans 8:37-39 (NIV)

My friend pauses to inhale. "Where are my days going? I am just trying to be a good wife and mom . . . and you are out speaking and writing books, and I don't know how you do it, and I know it's all a season, and what's it going to be like when this next little one comes? How our lives will change . . ." Deep breath, sigh. Mommy tiredness and mommy hope all in an exhale.

And then I see the other her, the one whose blog I read, whose voice inspires, whose message is resounding through the whole wide world. And I'm struck that my voice seems so . . . small. In between

119

carpools and doctor appointments, I glimpse yet another woman's speaking calendar, arena lights upon her, traveling the world saving a heart at a time, and I am so stilled at this moment that I'm actually grateful for her.

I'm thrilled I didn't miss my son's football season this year. To watch him and my husband (the Cowboy and the Coach) on their own Field of Dreams has been all this heart needed. I'm at home with my munchkins making pumpkin bread, harvest soup, memories. Blessed to not be on the road, on a plane, in another city ministering, when there is so much ministering to be done in my own backyard, kitchen, and upstairs rooms.

When I journal here, I want to put a face to all the longing: the longing for Enough. The house to be clean enough. There to be love enough. Our bodies to be good enough, in all their dimples, bumps and tucks. For us to look around and look inside and say, God, U R Enough, and in the mirror of Him we see crystal clear that so are we. Enough, that is. In all our "less thans," in all our longings, in all the laundry and linens and meetings and the search for More.

He says we are "More than Conquerors." That neither death nor life, neither angels nor demons, neither the present nor the future, nor any power in all Creation can separate us from the love of God that is in Christ. Nothing can separate us from His love for us! Nothing! Not past failures or post likes or popularity contests. Nothing in all Creation can separate us from His love. Therefore, we are More. More than Conquerors (Romans 8:37-39).

I am in the shower one morning and the voice of The Lord is clear, hot water pouring over achy body. "I am Enough for you, Jen."

These times with him, candle burning, coffee steaming, on the porch, view broadening: Enough. He is a still small voice breaking through a myriad of voices that compare. and comparisons only tell me my work in not enough. I am not enough. I should do more. I should be like her: More. (And we know Theodore Roosevelt said, "Comparison is the thief of joy.")

So in the Less of my life right now, in the Less rush, the Less deadlines, the Less traveling, and the Less worry, I am finding so much More. More women in my own community whose rich voices are a tune in my ear. More ways to give to those who live near and more time for those I love. I am finding more stillness in Less activity, and More joy in loving the One girl who's mine (four steps down the hall, one left). Loving her soul in all its stretches and shapes fills hours, weekends, a whole calendar . . . . I'm booked.

So wherever you are, at the top of your game, at the end of your valley, at the ridge of your life, or just the start of a journey . . . in the thick of it, in the Less of it, in the thinness, in the complexity or in the simplicity, right here, right now: God is Enough for you.

Once you see that clearly, look into His mirror: U R Enough too.

U R More than a conqueror.

Prayer

Dear Heavenly Father, I confess that YOU have already made me more than a conqueror. You aren't waiting around for me to conquer a bad habit, a besetting sin, or even that mound of laundry before I can be declared a conqueror. Instead, through the power of the cross you made me more than a conqueror. May I live out of who YOU say that I am and may I teach my children what this looks like so that they, too, might live from victory rather than striving to live to gain victory. In Jesus' Name, Amen.

FORTY

Honor

Lori Kennedy

Honor your father and mother, so that you may live long in the land the
Lord your God is giving you.

Exodus 20:12 (NIV)

The Ten Commandments are listed in Exodus Chapter 20. The first four are between us and God and the last six are between us and others. Honoring your mother and father is commandment number five, and it's the only commandment with a promise. It promises us a long life in the land the Lord our God is giving us should we keep this commandment.

I don't know about you, but I have struggled in this area. It's hard to say whether my struggles have been a result of my own broken lens from which I view and respond to the world, or of wrong responses that have been placed upon me by my parents and their broken views of themselves and the world. I have not understood what "honor" might look like and have not been sure how to respond if I feel, for example, that an unrealistic expectation has been placed upon me. I have always felt that no matter what I do, it is not good enough for my mother and that, no matter how I respond, I will not make her happy. So how, then, do I honor her? And, is she really placing expectations on me, or do I perceive expectations that don't really exist?

One day I got into an argument with my son before school. We got very angry with each other and he left the house for school with us both still very angry with each other. I took my anger to God and God showed me a precious nugget of His truth that day. First, He convicted me that my overreaction to my son's anger was a perceived rejection by him and that perception was why I lashed out so intensely. My prayers then turned to conviction of the broken lens through which I view the world. This lens says I'm not good enough and I'm not worthy. God has told me in His Word that this is a lie. In fact, He states it over and over and over again; I'm just a slow learner.

While I was aching over my sinful reaction to my child based on my unmet expectation of his response to me, I recognized the grief I was causing him and cried out to God that my flaws and sins not bleed through to my son. I want my child to know that he is loved and that he has great value to the Kingdom and in this world – despite me. I prayed that my stuff would not mess up my precious child.

In that moment in time, God revealed an amazing truth to me, and I understood the word "honor" in a new way as it referred to my mother and the real or perceived expectations in which I felt I never met. He showed me that the best way to honor my mother was to be true to the calling that God Himself has set before me and become the woman that He has called me to be! I realized in that instant that if my parents were healthy and whole (which no one is completely) then that's exactly what they would want for me. In this moment of my failure, God showed me that when we have true love and honor for others our desire is for them to do the will of the Father even when it might not seem best for us personally.

That simple but profound lesson has taken me leaps and bounds further in both my relationship and learning how to truly honor my mother as well as understanding my own flaws in my communications with my children as I continue to be molded by the Potter walking through this journey we call life.

Prayer

Dear Heavenly Father, you are such a generous and gracious parent. Thank you for speaking to each of us right where we are and for offering us the truth that sets our hearts free – free to love our children and our own parents without strings attached. May we honor you and others by living out of who you say we are. In Jesus' Name, Amen.

FORTY-ONE

The ONE Thing I Cannot Afford NOT to Make Time For

Katie Gibson

*Don't worry about anything; instead, pray about everything. Tell God what
you need, and thank him for all he has done. Then you will experience
God's peace, which exceeds anything we can understand. His peace will
guard your hearts and minds as you live in Christ Jesus.*

Philippians 4:6-7 (NLT)

I am right smack dab in the middle of the absolute craziest season
of my life. The absolute craziest, but the absolute best.

In between changing diapers, checking homework and trying to
figure out what kind of chicken I'm going to put on the dinner table I
have found I have to schedule evvvveryyyything.

I've got alarms, calendar events and to-do lists out the wazoo. My
life is crazy, but every now and again I come upon a week crazier than
all of the others. This has been one of those weeks.

125

This morning I woke up strangely coherent but noticeably "on edge" for 6 a.m. on a Monday morning, immediately remembering my lengthy to-do list with some tough-to-tackle items on it.

I r*aced* to get the kids dressed.

Raced to get out the door and in the car.

Raced—err . . . drove the speed limit, of course—to Pre-K with intentions to race my four-year-old to his class, hopeful that I could race home to squeeze in a quick workout.

No such luck.

My middle child decided today would be the first day in the history of EVER that he would cling to me as I turned to leave. Five minutes of hugs, kisses and high-fives later I was feeling flustered. I raced out of the school and back to my car only to find an e-mail on my phone, reminding me of another project that needed to move up on my to-do list.

I could feel the tension rising in my shoulders and creeping up my neck.

I *raced* home and *did* manage to get that workout in (I didn't manage to get a shower. Ew.), put baby B down for her nap, and was determined to conquer the big, scary List . . .

It was then that it dawned on me that I should spend some time talking to God and reading His Word. I made excuses: *I don't have time for that right now.*

The List was crying out, loudly.

I looked at the list. The list looked at me . . . I wanted to cry. *Seriously.* Determination crumbled. Anxiety and inadequacy overcame me. Doubt flooded in. *This is impossible. I need more time. I don't know how to take on that project. I can't do this.*

I reluctantly grabbed my Bible and curled up into the recliner. God I can't do this. I need your peace.

A few familiar words from today's verse popped into my mind. I looked it up and took in the timely words found in Philippians 4:6-7—'Tell God what you need...'

Yes, I can tell God what I need. I need peace. I need more time—no, I need more wisdom on how to use my time ... God, I don't know what I need, but I need something.

As I sat waiting I began to realize ... Jesus, you are peace. God, you are the author of time. You are wisdom ... God, I need more of you!

In just ten minutes my perspective had changed completely. I was no longer overwhelmed, no longer lacking—in time, peace, or wisdom. As I threw all my anxieties and inadequacies at Him, He dumped a truckload of peace on me.

I wish I could say that I'm awesome at spending quiet time with the Lord daily. I'm not awesome. Somehow, like Martha, I miss the fact that time spent at the feet of Jesus is not wasted time. Time and time again, I find myself on "E," walking—gas can in hand—back to my Savior.

But the truth I've found is this: The peace God gives is greater than any peace a checked box on my to-do list could ever offer.

And the bottom line is that I don't want to spend my life stressed. I don't want to be "on-edge" Mommy—liable to snap at any moment. I want to be deeply rooted in God's peace and presence so that I can gracefully handle anything life (or children) may throw at me.

Also, there is something rare, so captivating, about a peaceful spirit these days. It draws people to notice—"I want what you got"—

opening a window of opportunity to share Christ with an overextended and exhausted world.

We're busy, you and I, but let's put down our to-do lists and take a step of faith together, today.

The dishes can wait (it's hard, I know) and, let's face it, the laundry will never end anyway. Jesus is waiting on us to unload our cares on Him, so that he can dump His truckload of peace and wisdom on us in return. We can't afford NOT to make time for that!

Prayer

Dear God, help me to remember that time spent with you is more important and more fulfilling than checking off my to-do list. When I am anxious and weak, help me to turn to you, the source of true peace, wisdom, and abundant life. Help me continually fix my thoughts on things that are true, lovely, honorable, and worthy of praise, instead of lesser things that distract my mind. Thank you for your grace as I learn to still my soul and sit at your feet. In Your Name, Amen.

FORTY-TWO

Pick Up Some Rocks

Jill McSheehy

Then Jesus replied, "I assure you: The Son is not able to do anything on His
own, but only what He sees the Father doing. For whatever the Father does,
the Son also does these things in the same way.

John 15:9 (HCSB)

Alyssa had asked to ride her bike, so on this warm, August day when it was just the two of us, we headed out. I walked beside her, and my plan was for us to ride the length of our road and come back.

Suddenly, in the middle of her ride, Alyssa stopped. I had no idea why, so I watched as she walked over and picked up a small rock. "Hold this, Mommy, please. It's for my rock collection." In my hand was a plain gray rock, possibly only a fragment of the chip-and-seal. I held it and we continued.

A little further up, she stopped again, for the same reason. I marveled as she showed no concerns slowing her pace, taking her focus momentarily off her destination.

Besides drinking in the moment of enjoying this beautiful afternoon with her—my last year to have her home before she begins kindergarten—my sights were plainly set on the end of the road.

I'm so glad I didn't rush her. Because her simple act taught me something profound.

Sometimes I need to stop and pick up a rock.

I'm a "get to my destination" type of girl. Whether that is graduating college or making my sales goal in advertising or building a successful department in my career or organizing a new ministry at church, I see the destination, and I go forward.

But in my quest, do I see the rocks on my path, those individuals who might benefit from a pause in my run to pick them up?

Jesus had a destination, too. His destination was to die at the hands of men and rise from death. But what did he do in the days, weeks, months, and years preceding his destination?

He stopped to pick up rocks.

He saw beauty in ordinary sisters, longing in a tax collector, spark in a man born blind, potential in a simple fisherman.

He had his destination; from his Father's grand plan he never wavered.

But he still kept his eyes open on his path to see the rocks, especially the rocks cast aside by others.

And through those rocks he built his church, the unstoppable force of grace and truth for a dying and hurting world.

Prayer

Father, may I peel the blinders off my peripheral vision. May I slow my pace. I want my eyes be open to the rocks on the path. For they are more than rocks, of course. Each is unique, full of potential. And many are just longing for someone to stop and say, "Come with me; we've got an amazing destination ahead." In Jesus' Name, Amen.

FORTY-THREE

Up a Tree, Anyone?

Shellie Rushing Tomlinson

I sought the Lord and He heard me and delivered me from all my fears.

Psalm 34:4 (KJV)

Jessica Ann was playing on the carport while I prepared supper. I could see her easily through the screen door and still keep tabs on my youngest gumming crackers in his high chair. It was one of the first times I had allowed my three-year-old daughter outside without me but I was keeping a very close eye on her—or so I thought.

I was wiping Phillip's face when I heard the screams. It's been quite a few years now but this mama still remembers the fear in her voice. I flew for the door. "Mama's coming, Jess!" Horrible scenes instantly flooded my over active mind. Was my baby being threatened by a rabid dog? Had she wrecked her new tricycle and broken a bone? Was she bleeding? Good Lord, I hoped it wasn't a snake!

Yes, I was overreacting, but she was screaming—and this was my firstborn, people! Let's just say I was prepared to rescue her from the jaws of death, be it slippery reptile or hairy mammal. The rescue proved considerably less difficult.

Rounding the corner, I found my three-year-old stranded at the top of our carport like a baby kitten in a tree. Jessica Ann had climbed to the top of one of the supporting wrought iron poles and frozen. Obviously, the thrill had been totally in the ascent. All my poor baby could see now was the inside of the overhanging roof. With a firm touch on her feet and a reassuring voice, I coaxed the terrified explorer back down into my arms.

That long-ago rescue reminds me of a comforting promise from the Good Book.

Have you ever stared at the dead end of a road that once seemed to hold all the promise of a great adventure? Maybe such a plight isn't a memory for you. Maybe you're there right now. Tell me, are you holding on for dear life, trying to remember where it all went wrong? Are you up a creek without a paddle, up a pole without a ladder?

I might be having fun with the analogies, friends, but I couldn't be more serious about the solution. Psalms 34:4 says, *'I sought the Lord and He heard me and delivered me from all my fears."*

Please take a page out of Jessica's book. Give in and call out to the One who saves, heals, and delivers. The same God whose eye is on the sparrow is just a prayer away.

Prayer

Dear Heavenly Father, what a comfort it is to remember that your eye is on the sparrow and that you are watching over me and over my children. Give me the courage to let go of my perceived control and place my life and concerns in your very capable hands. In Jesus' Name, Amen.

FORTY-FOUR

A Table Set for Me

Sherri Sand

You prepare a table before me
in the presence of my enemies;
You anoint my head with oil;
My cup runs over.

Psalm 23:5 (NKJV)

Life's been hectic. Sick kids. Late nights. Too tired to get up for a quiet time with the Lord. But today I found myself on my knees and desperate for the Father's touch. Life's been so hard and I feel malnourished. Those still moments I steal away with my Father each morning feed my soul. They stock me full for the daily onslaught of attitudes gone sideways, children who don't always get along, and speed bumps in my race through the day.

Without those quiet times, I begin to feel like a refugee begging for a crumb from her Father's plate. But what I don't see, can't fully grasp in those impoverished moments is the banquet table He places before me.

There are platters piled high with grace, tureens of His bountiful love, trenchers overflowing with mercy and loaf upon loaf of forgiveness. His goodness and peace spill off the table He has set for me. There is no end to the bounty.

But when my eyes are too focused on my daily problems, and though I still crave His touch and long to taste the sweetness of His love, I forget that His table is so near.

Instead I seek solace from other sources. Hoping that a friend will offer the right words of comfort, or perhaps a shopping spree will clear my mind and perk me up. The "maybe-this-will-make-me-feel-better" list is endless.

But if I turn just so, I catch a glimpse of the table He's set for me. I run to it and eat hungrily, basking in His glory, His love and goodness that spill into my life and out to others. Life becomes amazingly wonderful once again and I feel safe-guarded in the minefield of life.

It's a table I need to visit daily. A Father I need to sit still before and lean against His knee or climb upon His lap. A table that meets all my needs and satisfies all my desires.

It's a table and a Father waiting for you.

Prayer

Dear Father, sometimes it is easy to forget that you have a table set just for me—where my needs are met and my appetites are satisfied. May I come to you first and may my children adopt this way of relating to you early on in their young lives as well. Thank you for making yourself to readily available to us! In Jesus' Name, Amen.

FORTY-FIVE

Why Would God Do That?

Tricia Williford

My frame was not hidden from You,
When I was made in secret,
And skillfully wrought in the lowest parts of the earth.
Your eyes saw my substance, being yet unformed.
And in Your book they all were written,
The days fashioned for me,
When as yet there were none of them.

Psalm 139:15-16 (NKJV)

I was reading to the boys from The Jesus Storybook Bible, which happens to be my very favorite version of Bible stories. These are far and above the best tellings of the stories that shape the foundation of what I believe. It's written for children, but good writing is good writing and I find myself falling in love with the stories all over again—or some for the first time—as I read them aloud to my children.

It was bedtime, and together we were reading the story of Abraham and Isaac. I was well into reading aloud before I realized that maybe this particular story is better processed during the day instead of bedtime—these images of a father climbing a hill with his young son, tying him down on an altar, and raising a knife to offer him as a sacrifice. My boys' eyes grew wider as we got closer and closer to the end of the story, and they breathed an audible exhale when we heard God relent at the last minute and spare Isaac's life.

This is at best one of the more troubling stories of the Old Testament. Tucker said, "I am so confused right now. Why would God do that? Why would God ask Abraham to kill his son?"

"Well, buddy, I don't understand this story completely, but I think it's because God had a very, very important job for Abraham to do. And he needed to know that Abraham would trust God and obey him, no matter what, even if it didn't make sense to him. And when he saw that Abraham would obey, then he didn't make him actually kill his son."

"So God rescued Isaac. And he didn't make Abraham give him up." I watched him trying to connect the dots.

"He did."

"Mommy, do you think you are like Abraham?"

Tyler interrupted. "Tucker, she doesn't want to kill us."

"I know that. It's not what I mean." He glanced to the ceiling in exasperation over the people in his life whom he must deal with. "But, Mommy, do you think God has an important job for you to do? And that's why he asked you to give up my dad?"

I had no words. Even now, as I remember him telling me his insight, I have no words.

In my silence, he continued. "Mommy, do you know God has picked you to write these books? He made you a writer to tell these stories. And so maybe God had to know you would trust him no matter what."

Good grief. Who is this child teaching me theology in my bedroom?

"But here's what I don't understand, Mom. If God rescued Isaac once he saw that Abraham would obey, why didn't he rescue my dad?"

Tucker was all questions, and Tyler was all ears right alongside his brother.

"I don't know, honey. I've asked God that question almost every day. Sometimes I get pretty angry with God over the whole thing."

He looked at me with pleading eyes, and his voice was gentle. "Mommy, no. Please don't be mad at God. I don't want you to go to hell."

"Oh, Tuck! That's not how it works, buddy. I won't go to hell for asking questions. God lets us feel how we feel, and he lets us ask him questions. In fact, there's a place in the Bible where David reminds us to tell God every one of our concerns. That means we can tell him anything we are feeling. And sometimes I miss your dad so much, and it makes me so sad that you don't have him, and I wish God would have made a different decision on that day. So I tell him."

It is impossibly heartbreaking to be so vulnerable in front of my children, to watch their faces reflect the conclusion that some of their greatest questions have no answers, to let them see that I just don't know.

"Come here, guys. Let me tell you something."

They climbed into bed with me. I wrapped my arms around them, and I told them what I think is true.

"You guys, your dad could have died twenty years ago. When he was in his sledding accident and his spleen ruptured, he could have died right then. But I think God thought to himself, 'If Robb Williford comes to heaven on this day, then Tricia Lott won't get to marry him.

And if Robb and Tricia don't get married, then Tucker and Tyler will never be born. I need those boys to be born because I need the world to have what they can bring.'"

My children were crying. I held them close, and I forged ahead. "I think God wants to show other people your friendship with each other. And he needs your hearts, and your tenderness, and your compassion. He needs you to play sports and tell stories. He needs you to make friends and love people. He wanted you here, so he let Robb Williford live long enough to become your dad."

"Really, Mommy?"

"Really. And I think he thought, I'll have Robb stay for another twenty years. It won't feel very long for Tricia, and it sure won't be very long for Tucker and Tyler, but it will be long enough for what I want to do."

"Are we here so Daddy could die?"

"No, baby. **I think he lived so you could be born.**"

"It makes me so sad, Mommy."

"I know, sugar. Me too."

I wrapped a blanket around the mound of us, and we cried. And I told God how we felt, right then and there so my boys could listen.

God, help me.

Prayer

Dear Heavenly Father, May my children have and enjoy an honest, authentic relationship with you and others because they see this modeled through my life and relationships. May we not give in to the pressure to be impressive, but may we live a life of freedom—where we walk in the grace you offer so freely, regardless of what may come. In Jesus' Name, Amen.

FORTY-SIX

The Family of God

Dorothy Johnson

Do not be afraid, for I am with you;
I will bring your children from the east and gather you from the west.

Isaiah 43:5 (NIV)

Read Ephesians 1: 3-6.

Some time ago, we were privileged to host a young Chinese-American woman for two months while she did an internship in our city. As part of getting acquainted, she and her parents told us the story of how God brought Jin Yao into their family eleven years before, when she was twelve years old.

It began with a disappointment. After going through a two-year process to adopt a girl from Vietnam, the day before they were to leave to pick her up, they were told that circumstances had changed, making the match impossible. But, there was a child in China who could be placed with them.

The couple and their son agreed to welcome the girl into their family. So they flew to China, met Jin Yao, and brought her home in a very short period of time. When I asked Jin Yao if she had been frightened about getting on an airplane with people she didn't know and flying halfway around the world, she replied, "It was a little scary. But I wanted a family."

Plus, she knew it was an answer to a prayer. You see, her faith journey actually began long before, when a man who came to the orphanage to play with the children told her about God. Even though the "mothers" said he was crazy and she shouldn't listen, she did and, as a result, offered up a simple prayer. "God, if you're there, send me a family." When He sent one, she didn't hesitate.

In talking about her adjustment to her new surroundings, Jin Yao mentioned that embraces and words of endearment were totally foreign to her because she had never been told she was loved. Consequently, at first, she didn't understand when her parents and brother wanted to hug her or what the words *I love you* meant.

I'm sure there were other moments that tried the patience and faith of everyone during Jin Yao's adjustment, for no family is perfect. However, the woman she has become is a wonderful testimony of God's faithfulness and her family's unconditional love.

I'm reminded that this little girl's story is an expression of eternal truths. The need to belong and to be valued as individuals is universal. And the way God answered Jin Yao's prayer is just one example of the lengths to which He will go to answer ours.

As believers, we're all adopted into the Family of God. When we come into it, we have to learn the ways of the family. Our brother, Jesus, shows us how to relate to one another. And we shouldn't worry if He changes our plans. Perhaps He wants us to be part of the answer to someone else's petition. When Jesus asks us to love sacrificially, it isn't always easy. But if we are willing, we will grow in grace and bring Him glory.

Prayer

Lord, help me convey your love to someone who is lonely and longing for acceptance. In Jesus' Name, Amen.

FORTY-SEVEN

The Power of Words

Jennifer Vander Klipp

The tongue has the power of life and death, and those who love it will eat its fruit.

Proverbs 18:21 (NIV)

When our children are young we spend a lot of time telling them what to do and what not to do. It's not surprising that many toddlers' first word is "No!" They hear it all the time! We use our words to teach our children what is dangerous, what is proper behavior, and, hopefully, to express how much we delight in them.

I think we all have experienced how life and death is in the tongue. We know how it feels to be cut us down with a thoughtless comment or having our day made with a meaningful compliment.

We know children need to be guided with words, but unless we're intentional about how we wield this power with other people we are missing opportunities to use words to bring life into our relationships. Here are some ideas for how you can bring life to those around you with your words and your improved relationship will be the fruit promised in Proverbs.

143

Praise what makes them unique. It's easy to say, "You're so nice." Or "You're such a good friend." But when you take the time to name what makes your friends unique—"You make the best desserts" or "You always know how to make me laugh"—you've shown that you pay attention to who they are as a person.

Ask their input. Sometimes the most powerful thing you can say is, "What do you think?" and then really listen to what they say. Don't formulate your response or get ready to argue why they're wrong. Value their opinion for what it represents as an aspect of your friend's personality or belief system. Let it give you some insight into who they are. The same goes for letting them pick the movie or the restaurant or any number of decisions. Learning to die to yourself is a great way to serve your family and friends and can bring you closer.

A close friend of mine has a rule that whenever he meets someone new, he asks them five questions about themselves before he says anything about himself. He has found this to be a wonderful ice breaker. When a person sees you as being genuinely interested in them as an individual, they open up and the conversation goes much more smoothly.

Actions speak louder than words. Sometimes an arm around a shoulder, a walk around the block, or just sitting quietly with a friend in a hospital room can be more powerful than speaking. There are times when your presence is all someone needs. Taking time out of your schedule to be present (really present—no electronics allowed) is one of the best gifts you can give to someone.

Prayer

Father, may I be known as one who speaks life into those close to me. Help me to do this for those you want me to build a closer relationship with.

Encourage them through me. Praise their uniqueness using my voice. Help me to challenge them to find their God-given passion. May I always remember that words are powerful and will have a lasting impact on them. In Jesus' Name, Amen.

FORTY-EIGHT

Believing I Am Fearfully and Wonderfully Made for the Sake of My Girls

Gillian Marchenko

I praise you because I am fearfully and wonderfully made; your works are wonderful, I know that full well.

Psalm 139:14 (NIV)

We took the kids to the pool a few days ago. I have four daughters, ages thirteen down to seven, and they were all excited about swimming. My husband and I claimed a spot on the pool deck and plunked down our stuff as the girls peeled off their bathing suit covers and tore towards the water.

I went to take of my cover, and paused. There I was, mom to all these girls of varying ages, thinking, *I don't want to take off my swim suit cover. I don't want people to see my flabby white legs, or my round bottom, or my Jello stomach.*

Oh, the plague of body image. It starts early. I remember being eleven years old, lean, tanned, and thinking I looked horrible. I hated my healthy, albeit slightly plump legs. I had a tiny pudge of a stomach, and I thought that every other girl and woman around me looked immensely better than I did.

Where did this come from? I don't remember my parents making a big deal out of my body. It's not like we had loads of fashion magazines lying around our house or that my mother put me on wonky diets as a kid. I was told I was pretty and loved.

But I just knew, somehow, early on, that the way my body looked mattered, and that I could never measure up to how I thought it should look, because my ideal would always be out of arm's reach. That's just humanity. That's just a warped perspective this side of the fall.

Now in my thirties my friends and I look back longingly for those days. "I can't believe we thought we were fat, or that it even mattered at that point if we were or not!" we proclaim in frustration.

And I am a mom. My body has been beat up through the years. My stomach is wobbly from growing babies. Stretch marks snake up my belly and curl around my thighs. I am at my heaviest weight to date, but regardless of all that, I know that I am loved, and that my body simply holds me, and that I have value. I am loved and desired by my husband. And I have these girls; all beautiful, all mostly uninhibited and unaware of the poor body image and inner struggle that tend to creep up in a woman's mind as she ages.

Right now their bodies aren't for show or for making people. They are to feel the cool water, to splash around, to enjoy. The girls look to me to set the tone. How does Mom feel about herself? Does she obsess about chubby arms and saggy skin on her neck? And so I work at it. I work to keep my negative thoughts about my body to myself. Although it is a struggle, I try to model health: eating, exercise, and general self-care. I try to love who I am and how I look because I am made in the image of God. I am fearfully and wonderfully made.

So, at the pool, I squared my shoulders, took a deep breath, and removed my swimsuit cover. I put on a smile, and walked towards my family in the pool, flabby, Jello-y, and happy.

We all had a great time that day. We swam and splashed and played for hours. And I don't think that anyone around us seemed to notice my flab. But I do hope they noticed my beautiful family. I hope they noticed that my girls were having fun and more importantly, that they had a mom unafraid to use the body God gave her to play with them at the neighborhood pool.

Prayer

Dear Heavenly Father, thank you for the reminders from you and from those who love us most that we are not our bodies—large or small, tall or short, muscular or petite, young or old. Thank you for these imperfect bodies that house the souls and spirits that will last forever. May we, as moms and sisters-in-Christ, affirm one another and remind one another that it's us you like—just the way we are. May we be free and may we pass this freedom on to our children and children's children. In Jesus' Name, Amen.

FORTY-NINE

Worth It

Katie Gibson

But God demonstrates his own love for us in this:
While we were still sinners, Christ died for us.

Romans 5:8 (NIV)

M otherhood makes me feel a bit invisible at times.

Sometimes I ask myself: *Does anyone hear me?*

Just this past week I had a full-fledged mommy meltdown about just that. There I sat, ugly-crying every bit of my pain, frustration, and mascara into a kitchen towel.

It wasn't exactly my proudest moment.

God often has to bring me to these places of brokenness to get me to spill out my junk so that He can help sort and trash. It's sort of like an internal episode of "Hoarders."

I brought my heartaches out, one by one . . .

God, I feel invisible. I feel like nobody cares. I feel like nobody sees everything I do, day in and day out. Being a mom is . . . tough.

I figured, if nothing else, it felt good to be honest.

But in that moment, I heard His compassionate voice break through my laments,

"Are you not worth more than many sparrows?"

I have to admit, I chuckled out loud. There, an emotional train wreck, dressed in second-day yoga pants, covered in toddler residue and about three days behind on work— *I didn't feel worth a Q-tip.* God's choice of scripture for that moment baffled me.

Worth. The word wouldn't stop echoing through the empty spaces of my soul.

I could feel God smiling on me, as light bulbs flickered on, one by one, enabling me to see the truth:

The crux of my pain and frustration was a seemingly unattainable goal I was striving to reach, yet it was something I possessed all along, and you have it too...

Worth.

Do you know how the value of an object is determined?

The answer is simple, right? *An item is worth what someone is willing to pay for it.*

In light of that question, think on this:

God, the Author and Creator of everything, did not spare *even His own son* for us (Rom. 8:32).

When we were held captive by the power of sin, Christ gave Himself as a ransom for us, bringing us into eternal life with Him (Matt. 20:28, Rom. 6:23).

The truth is that our worth is not based on what we do, or the things that we possess—our worth was securely established, once and for all, when God paid for us with His son's sacrifice.

However, we allow ourselves to be deceived and carry around the misbelief that if we have and do the right things and act a certain way, *then* we would be worthy, *then* people would see us.

Friend, your worth is not dictated by the numbers on a scale, your child's behavior, or even *your* behavior.

Your worth is not affected by the number of children under your roof, or the empty longing in your heart.

Your worth does not change based on whether you spend your days climbing corporate ladders, or cleaning up spills.

Your worth is not determined by what happened to you in the past, or how you *feel* in the present.

Your worth does not fluctuate based on what others said to you, *or didn't*.

Your worth does not increase if you can cook, craft, clean, breast-feed, run 3.1 miles or hold your temper . . . *and neither does it decrease if you cannot.*

The Father is saying to us today, *"Stop wearing yourself out for worth."*

We are already deeply loved and dearly valued. It's time to eradicate our misconceptions with the truth of God's Word. We must learn to abide in the place of *worthiness*, in Christ. The place where all of the pressure is removed, and all of our worries and fears about measuring up are stamped "null and void" under the truth that God says we are *worth it.*

If you're feeling unnoticed, unloved or undervalued today, remember that you are far more valuable than many sparrows, and God's word says that not one of them falls to the ground without Him knowing (Matt. 10:29). God sees you, right where you are, and just as you are, and He *delights* in you.

No matter what, you are loved, you are treasured and you are *worth it*.

Prayer

Father, thank you for your immeasurable love. Forgive me for wearing myself out for what was right in front of me all along—the worth you bestowed on me when you gave your Son's life for mine, purchasing eternal life on my behalf. Help me to learn how to abide in that place of worthiness. Thank you that I am fully known and infinitely treasured in You. Amen.

FIFTY

Role Reversal

Deb DeArmond

Honor your father and mother ...

Exodus 20:12 (NIV)

A recent late night discussion with one of my sons reminded me how things change as we grow older.

"I'm really proud of you, Mom. At this stage of life, it would be easy to slow down and cut back. You are moving ahead with some new and exciting things God's placed on your plate. It's awesome – and I'm praying for you."

It made me smile. His phrase, tossed in my direction, *at this stage of life*, meant, *as you grow older*. A really polite way of pointing that out. It made me smile, too, because it was an encouraging expression of his support—which I appreciate greatly.

It also touched my *heart*, because it sounded familiar. *Parental.* "I'm really proud of you." How many times in my life had I said those exact words to my son and his brothers?

And in that moment, I realized, that the roles would continue to shift over the coming years.

My mother, at 84, used to say to me, "Remember who the parent is in this relationship, Dear." That was her gentle reminder that the tone or words I had used made her feel like a child – even though it was not my intent. She knew she needed more help each day, with tasks and chores she had once done without a second thought. But she wanted to remain *who she was* right up until the end – my mother.

I'm not 84. I have a very long way to go to reach that point, but this moment with my son put me on notice: children often become their parents' counselors, drivers, healthcare advocates, financial advisors (and sometimes providers) and so much more. The baton passes and the roles realign. It's "the circle of life" I suppose.

I'm grateful to say that at the moment, my sons are not in these roles. They are my cheerleaders and champions. It's wonderful to have them waving me on and celebrating achievements along with me.

My prayer is that I go home to be with Jesus before the time comes that I need a caregiver. If that is not God's plan, I am grateful and confident in my sons and their wives that they will live fully the charge in God's Word.

Honoring father and mother is not a suggestion. It's one of the Big Ten, and it's not always easy to do. Some may find themselves taking care of kids and Mom and/or Dad at the same time. Juggling soccer practice and hip replacement specialists at the same time is overwhelming.

It is a conscious choice we will make when the time comes. Not all children are willing to take on the eldercare role. The evening news is unfortunately filled with stories of neglect and abuse of the elderly— emotional and physical. Some seniors fall prey to their children and suffer financial loss to sons or daughters who treat Mom's finances as their own and spend that which was meant to provide for a parent's later years.

The Lord has an opinion about this and He has a special place in His heart for the widow, in particular. He calls caring for the orphans and widows in their trouble as "pure and undefiled religion," James 1:27 (NKJV).

Three additional scripture references:

"Listen to your father, who gave you life, and don't despise your mother when she is old," Proverbs 23:22 (NLT).

"For instance, God says, 'Honor your father and mother,' and 'Anyone who speaks disrespectfully of father or mother must be put to death.'" Matthew 15:4 (NLT).

"If you honor your father and mother, "things will go well for you, and you will have a long life on the earth," Ephesians 6:3 (NLT).

So if today, if you find yourself struggling with the responsibility as a child of parents in need of care and support, bind the words of the Lord to your heart. He knew you would play this role. He saw it before you did. And He has equipped and empowered you to withstand it. Even on days when it seems impossible, it isn't, as long as you do it in Him.

Prayer

Dear Heavenly Father, Thank you for my parents and for my children. I pray that this principle of honoring our parents would be found to be consistent in how I live my life and that your wisdom would guide my steps in how this looks specifically in my life, my circumstances and the seasons as they inevitably change. In Jesus' Name, Amen.

FIFTY-ONE

Trust and Obey

Kristan Dooley

What is more pleasing to the Lord; your burnt offerings and sacrifices or your obedience to His voice?

I Samuel 15:22 (NLT)

Read Ephesians 5:1-7.

Ephesians has helped me so much these past few weeks. I love what I'm learning and I love how much the Father is using it as we venture to a new level of intimacy and trust. The deeper our love grows, the easier it is to surrender and obey. Surrender and obedience always leads to blessing. He has such amazing things in store for those of us who are willing to follow.

What stood out to me ...

The absolute first thing grabbing my attention is the second statement in verse 2, "He loved us and offered himself as a sacrifice for us, a pleasing aroma to God." This statement reminds me of a passage of Scripture in 1 Samuel 15, "What is more pleasing to the Lord; your burnt offerings and sacrifices or your obedience to His voice?" (verse 22).

Jesus offered himself as a sacrifice because his heart was to be obedient to the Father's plan. He knew what was coming and it's safe to say he wasn't looking forward to it. He even asked for it to be removed. "If there were any other way, please, Father, take this cup from me," (Luke 22:42). No one wants to die. Death isn't ever easy! But the truth is, there isn't any other way. In the end, Jesus surrendered and obedience pushed him to climb the hill to Calvary where he would die for the sins of the world.

Obedience is hard, it's costly, it takes a commitment, but it is also deeply rewarding and extremely profitable (both for us and for the Kingdom!). I love the picture I get in my head when I think about my sacrifice of obedience being a sweet aroma to God. The picture of a beautiful smell making its way to Him gets me excited. I imagine He would inhale deeply and breathe out, richly satisfied with the desires of my heart.

The conversations around the Dooley house have been interesting this summer. My girls are growing up. They are past the point of simply accepting my answers because they come out of my mouth. "But, why," has finally made its annoying appearance and, man, it is all over the place. "But why, Mama?" There little minds just want to know. They can't take it! They must know and understand why they are doing what I've asked them to do. And I get it, it's always nice to understand why we are doing what we are doing—but it's not always necessary. Answers aren't necessary, trust is. Their level of trust in me and my heart for their well-being should leave them without the worries of the why.

Sometimes I answer them and other times I pause and ask, "Do you trust me?" To which they mostly say, "Yes, Mom." (Although asking them this question has caused me to ask myself, "Have I given them ample reason to trust me?" Which is really good accountability.) After their little "Yes," I follow up with, "Then trust what I've asked you to do or not to do is in your best interest."

It doesn't mean they don't ever get answers. Sometimes there are very simple answers to questions like, "Why do we have to go to bed at 9 p.m. in the middle of the summer?" But other times, I don't have answers they would ever fully understand, even if I shared them. Sometimes all I can say is that it's because I truly believe it is in their best interest. Even when they don't see it, even when they don't understand, even when it would appear easier to let it unfold differently.

I think this reflects the heart of the Father. He has such good things in store for us. Things we can't even begin to see or grasp or fully understand. If we will have hearts committed to obedience without needing full understanding, He promises to get us there. It's not only about knowing, it's also about doing, but the two are directly related. We do because we know, we don't know in order to do. Because we know and trust the heart of our Father, we can submit and obey His instructions. Flipping the equation leaves us working to earn His favor instead of resting in the favor He has already promised. He doesn't want us to sacrifice on the altar of sacrifice. He wants us to sacrifice on the altar of obedience.

"If you are willing and obedient, you shall eat the good of the land." (Isaiah 1:19)

"As the Father has loved me, so have I loved you. Abide in my love. If you keep my commandments, you will abide in my love, just as I have kept my Father's commandments and abide in his love." (John 15:9-10)

At some point in the game, love is about surrender and obedience. It is about letting go of ourselves and holding on to Him. Jesus let go of himself so He could hold on to the Father and through His sacrifice and obedience we were gifted eternity. No doubt, the biggest blessings live just on the other side of our surrender and obedience.

Prayer

I will give (all that I know of myself, my time, my passions) when it's easy. I will give when it's hard. I will give when it makes sense. I will give when it doesn't. I will give. What I have is yours. My biggest desire is to be obedient to your voice—without hesitation, without doubt, without fear. Simply because of the level of trust between the two of us. I know your heart is so for me, Father. I know you hold me in your hands and delight in my presence. May that be enough for me to bow my knee in faithful surrender. In Jesus' Name, Amen.

FIFTY-TWO

When Motherhood Is a Mirror

Jessica Wolstenholm

Her children rise up and call her blessed.

Proverbs 31:28 (ESV)

Lately, I've not been able to utter a word without hearing my mother's voice. In the last six months I've realized how much I sound like her. She echoes each word I say as if she were standing right next to me, in every mothering moment. Since losing her eighteen months ago, she dwells within the caverns of my mind and now, she surfaces each time I speak.

For the most part, her echo is comforting, as I hope to emulate the very best of my mother's wisdom. At times though, it's heartbreaking, as I wish for one more conversation, one more phone call, even one last nagging lecture.

Her voice has become a part of me, and through my own I am reminded of her constant presence. My words become her legacy as I seek to mirror not only her voice but her deep, deep love as well.

My voice is a mirror of my mother's and so is my face. I've heard others remark that the resemblance is uncanny. I look just like her when she was my age. I often gaze at photos of her later in life, peering into my future face. I don't mind being a walking reflection of my mother. She was radiant, lighting up every room she entered with her love. Motherhood is a mirror and I have a beautiful legacy to reflect.

I watch my own reflection, walking around in the body of a seven-year-old. She has my eyes ... my smile ... my pointy chin. But her appearance is only the tip of the iceberg of similarity. She has my free spirit, my lack of focus, that overwhelming need to be active and creative. She is everything of me that is good and beautiful and a walking reminder of each weakness I hold. Each thing about her that drives me crazy is but a reflection of that which makes me tire of myself.

Motherhood is a mirror and I peer daily into the depths of what I could be ... what she could be ... if only we could overcome that which holds us back.

I long to be able to ask my mother what it was like to watch a smaller, younger version of herself go through life. I imagine she'd tell me to lead her gently; to let compassion and grace be my guides as I help her navigate past the weaknesses I am just now coming to understand. She'd tell me to be patient with my mini-me, because some day those things that frustrate me will become her greatest strengths with my help.

My mother would look deep into her own mirror with great pride. She'd recount every way my girl is a beautiful reflection of me, and encourage me to love her beyond myself.

Motherhood is a mirror. An opportunity to catch a glimpse of ourselves as we stand in front of the ones we've given life. It's the blessing that allows us to reflect on the best of who we are and impart her to those that will carry our legacy.

Prayer

Dear Heavenly Father, as we look into the mirror of motherhood, I pray that we will find ourselves reflecting your character more and more—and that we will impart that image to our children as well. In Jesus' Name, Amen.

FIFTY-THREE

Weddings

Jan Dunlap

Love is patient, love is kind. It does not envy, it does not boast, it is not proud. It does not dishonor others, it is not self-seeking, it is not easily angered, it keeps no record of wrongs. Love does not delight in evil but rejoices with the truth. It always protects, always trusts, always hopes, always perseveres.
Love never fails.

I Corinthians 13:4-8 (NIV)

I'm watching my son and his new bride spin around the dance floor. They are blissfully happy, and so am I, because I know this is a good, strong marriage they are celebrating tonight. That's not to say the last few weeks have been carefree, however.

The weeks of preparation are behind them now, as are the last-minute panics about the change in venue for the ceremony (the scheduler unwittingly double-booked the park overlook), the invitations that were lost in the mail, and the wrong flowers in the bouquets. Those things aren't important anymore, and while they caused my son and (now) daughter-in-law some stressful moments, I know they've already forgotten them (or at least, they will be able to laugh about them in the near future . . . I hope).

What is important is their love for each other, and the faith that their love can endure all things. As an old married lady myself (my marriage will be thirty-seven years old this December), I know that no one can predict all the twists and turns and straightaways that lay ahead of every newlywed couple; I also know that not every marriage can survive the journey. But what I do know is that when God is welcome in a couple's life, "love never fails." (I Corinthians 13:8).

And so that is my prayer for my son and his bride as they dance on their wedding night—and for every couple who summon the faith and hope to say "I do" to each other—that they will invite Christ into their marriage.

After all, we all know what happens when Jesus gets invited to a wedding . . .

Prayer

Dear Heavenly Father, as my children grow into adulthood and as they form strong attachments to others, especially in regard to romance and marriage, I pray that it would be your love that would bind their hearts in commitment to one another. In Jesus' Name, Amen.

FIFTY-FOUR

Hold Still and Open Up

Anita Agers-Brooks

We do not want you to become lazy, but to imitate those who through faith
and patience inherit what has been promised.

Hebrews 6:12 (NIV)

I f you've given birth and raised children, this may resonate. If you've ever watched a parent attempt to feed a small child, you might chuckle—or cringe.

When my grown men were little guys, especially in that three-to-eight-month-old stage, most feedings were a wrestling match. It went something like this.

"Look what mommy's got for you," I'd say.

At first, when their bellies growled from hunger, they eagerly accepted what I had to offer. Too eagerly.

Trying to outmaneuver me, they lunged toward the spoon. In their crazed enthusiasm, it wasn't uncommon for them to writhe and twist, often causing a pile of pureed peas to land in an ear, a cache of carrots to go up their nostril, or a lump of applesauce to dump in an eye.

Sometimes laughing, sometimes frustrated, I would say, "Hold still, you're making a mess. If you'd wait for me, I could feed you easier."

But they seldom listened. By the time we were done, they wore a slathering of food, and missed out on the relaxed pleasure of a tasty, nutritional meal.

When they became bored or temporarily full, my children avoided eye contact, grunted, and clamped their lips in a show of defiance. No matter how much I coaxed.

"Eat it, it's good for you. I'm going to give you what I'm offering anyway, so why insist on making things messier than they need to be? Hold still and open up."

This makes me think about God as our parent. I wonder how often He looks on us with love, cooing and coaxing, "I'm going to give you what you need anyway. Hold still, open up, and receive it. Don't make things unnecessarily messy. Enjoy what I have to offer."

But we in our impatience, lunge, twist, writhe, trying to get what we want, slathering ourselves with gook as we go.

When we think we've gotten all we need from Him, our stubborn nature steps up. We avoid eye contact, grunt, clamp our lips and attempt to turn away.

Thankfully, God is a parent. He doesn't refuse to feed us again. He never stops offering us tasty nutrition. He's even willing to clean up the messes that we make. If we would just hold still and open up.

Over time, my children learned a bit more patience, saving us time and energy. As adults, they've discovered stubbornness only makes things harder on them.

These are the same lessons I'm striving to learn in my relationship with my Daddy God. Hebrews 6:12 (NIV) says, "*We do not want you to become lazy, but to imitate those who through faith and patience inherit what has been promised.*"

Our Father promises us good things, on a daily basis He holds out His gifts and says, "Look what Daddy's got for you."

It's up to us to hold still and open up.

Prayer

Father God, we often make the biggest messes, don't we? You're only offering us what is best and in our immaturity and insecurity, we get in our own way. This is so easy to see in our own children, but so difficult to see in the mirror. Thank you for your patience with us ... with me. Here am I, holding still and opening up to whatever it is you have for me today. In Jesus' Name, Amen.

FIFTY-FIVE

Story Power

Karen Jordan

Write down for the coming generation what the LORD has done, so that people not yet born will praise him.

Psalm 102:18 (GNT)

Would you like to read your great-great grandmother's journal about her immigration to America? What about your father's love letters to your mother from the trenches of the battlefield? Would you cherish the private diaries that your grandmother kept next to her bed, where she wrote down the intimate details of her life?

I would! But often the people that we love the most do not know the stories that matter most to us.

Recording History

If I don't write down my family stories, my grandchildren may never know why we moved our family from Texas in 1980 in response to our faith. Nor would they know why I continue to encourage others to write the stories that matter most.

168

I would love to know more of my family's history, but very few of them left any written records. I have no way of identifying the people and places in some of our family photos, because both of my parents and extended family are gone. I only know what I've read on my ancestors' gravestones—their names, birth and death dates, and a few interesting epitaphs.

Considering Epitaphs

As I read this epitaph as a teenager, I also noticed the ceramic photo of the deceased on his headstone: "Beware kind friend as you pass by, where you are now, so once was I. Where I am now, you soon shall be. Prepare for death and follow me."

I referred to this inscription several times in the past few years. I quoted it when teaching composition at UALR, as my students began their academic journeys. Later, I shared it with some new writing teachers. And I hope it encourages you to record your faith and family stories.

My mother composed her own epitaph, but she didn't know it at the time. We engraved a quote from one of her poems on her headstone. She wrote, "Happiness, joy, God's promise I find. My search has now ended, salvation is mine" (Nelle Baize, 2001).

Building Legacies

My mother left us her collection of poems as part of her legacy. When Mother read her words to me for the first time during a long-distance phone call, a new voice emerged from her poetry—a voice of hope, love, and faith.

After Mother died, I realized that no one else in my family knew about her poetry. My brother and two sisters knew many of our family stories. But Mother never told her most powerful faith stories—like the account of her spiritual transformation after her heart stopped during a medical procedure. And now, she could not share her miraculous testimony of deliverance and healing that had touched my heart and transformed my concept of heaven and hell.

Psalm 102:18 also encourages us, "Write down for the coming generation what the LORD has done, so that people not yet born will praise him" (GNT).

Remember, when we begin to tell the stories that matter most, lives change and hearts heal—that's Story Power!

Prayer

Father, thank you for our stories, which are powerful. May we never diminish our own stories nor neglect to pass testimonies of Your faithfulness on to the next generation – and especially to our own children. Give us creative ways to help them remember these stories and, in turn, begin the practice of passing along their own stories to others.

FIFTY-SIX

Feeling Out of Your League?

Cindi McMenamin

If any of you lacks wisdom, you should ask God, who gives generously to all without finding fault, and it will be given to you.

James 1:5 (NIV)

Do you ever have those days when you doubt your abilities as a mom?

I remember feeling way out of my league as a mom—especially when my daughter hit the teenage years. I was still trying to figure out how to instill healthy values in her, how to enforce the rules in our home, and how to be reasonable, not legalistic, when it came to listening to her, even if what she wanted to do or wear was not my personal preference.

So many times I found myself saying, "I'm still trying to figure this out. I've never been a mom to a teenager before."

Now *that* must have given her an extra dose of confidence in me! Looking back on those years now, Dana wasn't really a challenge at all. I was just trying to be the best mom I could and felt like I was failing through most of it. Oh, how I wish I knew back then what I know now.

Now that my Dana is twenty-two years old and has turned into quite a lovely lady, I realize that half of what freaked me out wasn't so important in the long run. I was comparing myself to other moms who were in different situations than me. I was feeling imperfect based on a set of expectations that were mine, not my child's. And I was failing to remember that God had appointed *me* to be my daughter's mother because He knew how desperately I'd need to depend on Him to get me through. And, God has been faithful every step of the way.

Parenting can be scary when we see our children make choices we wouldn't have made, when they start walking a path that looks uncertain to us, or when they no longer want our opinion or watchful eye on them. We struggle through the memory of them clinging to our legs, only to see them running with all their might to get away from our arms. And yet . . . the God who made you mother of each of your children didn't make a mistake. He knew exactly what you were capable—and incapable—of. And He stands ready to be your Right Hand Man as soon as you call to Him for help.

In Psalm 16:8, David the Psalmist said, *"I have set the Lord always before me. Because he is at my right hand, I will not be shaken."* Have you ever thought about that? God is at your right hand, too, whispering wisdom, offering comfort, and providing peace just when you need it. And for those times you don't feel qualified? Call upon your Right-Hand Man.

In James 1:5 we are told:

"If any of you lacks wisdom, you should ask God, who gives generously to all without finding fault, and it will be given to you."

That tells me that our Right-Hand Man is waiting to help us, generously, and without finding fault in what we're doing. When you're mothering and feeling out of your league, that is priceless. When you are depending on God to get through whatever lies ahead in parenting, God has you right where He wants you to be. Cling to Him. It is there you'll find wisdom, direction, support, comfort, and most all, your sanity.

Prayer

Heavenly Father, it is often easier to get caught up in the comparison trap and feel overwhelmed with responsibility than it can be to find our rest and strength in You. Thank you for this reminder that You are always with us and that we do not go it alone as moms. Thank you for loving us right where we are and not being a fault-finder as you examine our lives. What grace! In Jesus' Name, Amen.

FIFTY-SEVEN

Blessed Is She . . .

Jennifer Strickland

Blessed is she who has believed that the Lord would fulfill his promises to her!

Luke 1:45 (NLT)

Mary. The mother of God. The Sinless one. The Holy one. The Blessed Virgin. History has painted Mary as perfect. Having a Queen in Heaven who advocates on our behalf has been remarkably helpful for countless women. Since I was not brought up with religion, however, I have only the Scriptures to define what the mother of Jesus was like. Regardless of how history has framed her, the perfect Word reveals she is more like us than we might imagine.

According to Luke, she was a girl from Nazareth and a virgin engaged to be married to a carpenter. Reading her famous Magnificat (Luke 1:46-55) reveals that the history of her people and her God were seared on Mary's heart. Many have claimed that she was blessed with being the mother of the Messiah because of her purity, reverence, and holiness. Certainly she was highly favored with God, in the words of the angel Gabriel. But let's read what Elizabeth, her dear friend, exclaimed upon hearing Mary was pregnant with the Christ: Blessed is she who . . . Remains a virgin forever? Never sins? Never questions God? Memorizes Scripture? No, Elizabeth cried out some of the most profound words women claim in all of Scripture: Blessed is she who has believed that what the Lord has said to her will be accomplished! Blessed is she who has believed.

When the angel Gabriel first approached her, Mary was greatly troubled. And when he told her that she would be the mother of the Son of God, she definitely questioned it. How could this be, for I am a virgin? She asked.

Nothing is impossible with God, the angel told Mary.

Mary answered with the words God must long to hear from all of us: I am the Lord's servant, she responded, "May it be to me as you have said." And as any woman would do, she hurried to tell a friend. She and Elizabeth excitedly exchanged news, and Mary broke out in her song of praise, the Magnificat: "From now on all generations will call me blessed."

Unfortunately women over time have felt disconnected from Mary. She has seemed too perfect. We cannot relate to someone who never sinned and whose son never sinned. History's framing of her as an eternal virgin is just too unrelatable. And yet, the Scriptures reveal that not only did she bear more children, but that she also needed a Savior: "My soul glorifies the Lord and my spirit rejoices in God my Savior," she said. She was as human and as in need of God as the rest of us. What is different about her, in the angel's words, is that she was highly favored with God. This is the part that draws me to her, because I (like most of us) want blessing and favor with God.

Like Abraham, Mary's faith was credited to her as righteousness. It wasn't that she did everything right – in fact at the wedding at Cana she got on Jesus' nerves a bit as she attempted to nudge him into public ministry. Later, while the crowds pushed against him, she sent someone in to get him, but he disregarded her call, remaining with the people who needed to hear his teaching most. Nevertheless, she was there outside the door (confused and afraid most likely) but ever faithful.

At Jesus' baby dedication at the temple, the prophet Simeon turned to Mary and said that Jesus' life would cause the rise and fall of many, and a sword would pierce her own soul too. At the cross, these words became an ominous foretelling of their fate: before her eyes her son was beaten and crucified by the very people he came to save. The child who had been born in her arms had grown into a man spat upon and despised by so many. Knowing he was God's one and only Son must have caused her immeasurable sorrow. But when nearly all his disciples had run away in terror, faithful Mary remained at the foot of the cross until he gasped his last breath. Even after Jesus had returned to the Father, she gathered with all the believers in prayer.

The fact that she believed does not mean that she didn't question, didn't doubt, didn't grieve and worry. But the fact that she believed was the source of her blessedness. The good news for us is that Scriptures show no evidence of her perfection, only her faith. 1 Peter 3:5 says the women of the past used to make themselves beautiful by putting their hope in God. To me, this is what makes Mary so beautiful: her hope.

Sometimes I want so badly to do something great. I see the suffering in the world and I want to solve it. But then I remember Mary. She simply opened herself as a vessel of His Spirit. Despite all questions, she believed. She allowed Christ to come inside of her, dwell and grow within her, literally. And from that faith was born the hope of the world.

What are you questioning God about right now? What makes you doubt? What makes you worry? Remember Mary. Open your heart as she opened her womb. Allow God's plans to grow within you. Trust Him. From your faith great things can come. For it is only in the growth of His Spirit within us that real miracles are born. And through us, yes, God can touch suffering—and heal it.

Blessed is she who has believed.

Prayer

Lord, I believe. Help my unbelief!*

*Mark 9:24

FIFTY-EIGHT

Epic Mom Fail

Jennifer Vander Klipp

*And we know that God causes all things to work together for good to those
who love God, to those who are called according to His purpose.*

Romans 8:28 (NASB)

S ometimes as a mom you have those situations that slam your
self-confidence. Sometimes you do things that you're sure will
give your kids great fodder for a tell-all novel someday. It's usually not
as bad as all that, but in the moment you feel like you should get the
worst mom award. I'll share two of them, both involving my son, who
seems no worse for my failures.

My son was a preschooler and we were living in Arizona. He and
I had just finished returning books to the library, the last on a long list
of errands that day, and had gotten back into the minivan. I buckled
my son in, tossed all my stuff on the front seat, and closed the door. I
went around to get in my side.

The door was locked.

Through the window I could see all the doors were locked, but I
still pulled on the door handle like somehow reality would change. I

178

could see the keys sitting on the driver's seat, along with my purse and cell phone.

I knew my son could unlock the doors. Except that he was strapped in his car seat. However, childproof things had never deterred him before. I told him how to get himself out of his seat. "Just push that red button." He poked at it, sucker in his mouth. Then he pushed harder, but he just didn't have the strength to get it. We tried seeing if he could unbuckle the car seatbelt and free the car seat, but he couldn't reach it.

I was going to have to call and get help. But my phone was in the car, too, so I had to leave him to go back into the library. It went against every instinct to leave my son alone in a car while I went inside. But, I thought, if someone could break into the car to steal it (and who wants a 1998 minivan with 180,000 miles on it?) I could at least get my son out. So I hurried inside to find a pay phone. Apparently pay phones didn't exist anymore. I finally asked the librarian.

She laughed. "Oh, I don't think it works."

Not funny. "I need a phone. I've locked my keys in the car with my son. I need to call somebody."

"Oh, I guess you can use this then." She moved her desk phone toward me. I called AAA and went through the whole explanation of how I couldn't supply them my membership card number because it was in my purse, which was locked in my car with my son.

On my way back to the car, there was this guy who had been outside the library trying to get people to sign his petition. I didn't know what for, and I didn't care. He'd seen me walk by now four times and started pestering me to sign his stupid petition.

"I'm a little busy right now."

"Doing what?"

Oh, the things that went through my mind. I didn't say any of them, however. Let's just say that the next time I need to write a dead body in a book it will be a guy that looks a lot like him trying to get people to sign a petition. I just kept walking to the van where I hoped my son wasn't a sobbing, hysterical mess. I peered in the window. He was frowning, but I think that was because he had dropped his sucker.

So I leaned my head against this really dirty window—when was the last time I washed this thing anyway?—and talked to him. People driving through the parking lot stared at me. What was this crazy woman doing talking to a car? A police officer drove by. I watched him, half hoping he'd stop. He didn't. I told my son to go to sleep, and for once in his life, he minded me.

I was really thankful it was only the upper 60s and not 112 degrees. I started thinking which window would be the cheapest to replace and looked around for a big rock. Nothing. If it were 112, I had no idea what I could have used to break the window. Well, he was asleep, AAA was on the way, and other than people thinking I was nuts, there wasn't any problem with waiting. Just that my daughter got out of school in thirty minutes and since our neighbors had moved, there wasn't a house for her to go to if I wasn't home.

After about twenty-five minutes a tow truck pulled into the parking lot. The guy got out with all his equipment. Then he saw my son. "Hey, if we'd known there was a kid in the car we would have gotten here in five minutes. Why didn't you tell us?"

I'm pretty sure I mentioned it.

The guy started prying open the door with this little inflatable device. Very cool, though frankly I didn't care if he ripped the door off.

The door opened. My son woke up. The tow truck guy packed up his stuff.

I thought I would throw up.

It's about nine years before the next trauma involving my son and locks.

When he was eleven, my son got dropped off at home from school one day only to find the door locked and his key and his phone in the house. None of the stay-at-home neighbors had stayed at home that day. And it was 17 degrees out.

I drove up an hour later to find him sobbing, crying ice cubes, as he told me later. He'd kept himself busy trying to pick the lock with a stick, opening the garage to see if he could start the barbecue (so glad he couldn't!), and kicking snow off the porch.

This one was sort of his fault. He knew to the keep the key in his backpack, but remembering is not a strong suit of Asperger's kids. And if I'd thought about it, I'd have left the side door open. But with my daughter in the hospital with a juvenile arthritis flare up, I wasn't thinking too clearly either.

So from the desert of Arizona to the upper Midwest, I'm capable of the epic Mom fail. Somehow my children survive my best attempts to raise them properly.

Our kids actually learn something from our failures. They learn that we aren't perfect. Which may not be a revelation to us, but it is to our kids. Do you remember the first time you realized your parents made a mistake? For most of us that was a profound moment.

Our kids learn how to handle mistakes by how we handle ours. Do we get upset or angry beyond reason? Do we ask for forgiveness? Do we see what we can learn from the situation?

Let's remember more is caught than taught. And you've given them some great stories to tell your grandkids someday.

Prayer

God, sometimes it feels as though I fail in unique ways. It can seem as though other moms somehow keep it all together while I feel like I'm falling apart. Thank you for this reminder that we're all a mess—we're all just doing the best way can—and when we fail, which we will, you're already in the business of working it all together for something good. I praise you for who you are and what you've done and what you're presently doing. In Jesus' Name, Amen.

FIFTY-NINE

Feeling Exhausted?

Cindi McMenamin

So teach us to number our days, that we may present to You a heart of
wisdom.

Psalm 90:12 (NASB)

A mom of two toddlers recently asked me for advice on those
days when she has a hard time just getting out of bed and getting going.

I remember those days, feeling life was taking a lot out of me; feeling my child needed so much from me. And, at times, feeling I had so
little left to give. I survived those days by taking some advice from
Moses in Psalm 90:12. It was a simple prayer of his that refocused me
on what was most important and warned me not to wish away that
season of life too quickly: *"So teach us to number our days, that we may*
present to You a heart of wisdom."

It's natural, at times when our children are young, to want to stay
under the covers and not face the day, especially when you feel like
getting out of bed will result in feeling run down. But our altitude

(how high we can keep our spirits, or how low we can sink in motivation or despair) is directly affected by our attitude. So, we need to remember the reason we still live, breathe and have our being.

We were created to love God and enjoy Him forever. He's given us certain blessings that we only have so long on this earth to enjoy. So when life starts to feel like drudgery, we must "number our days" so we can live wisely. As you lie in bed, tired mom, searching for your motivation to get up and get going, here are some facts you can focus on that will help you number your days:

Life is short. Make these twelve hours of daylight count by doing at least one thing you've never done before.

Your children are growing fast. Do something with them today that they will remember throughout their childhood.

You aren't guaranteed a tomorrow . . . for yourself or your children. What one thing can you do to make this day stand out in your mind—and theirs—as a gift from God?

You are on a limited-time assignment. God has given you a task to raise these children and it will be over in a matter of years that will race by like seconds. Study them today. Memorize their little faces. Take notes on what you observe. Make every moment with them count.

And once those reminders drive you out of bed, here are some practical things you can do to maintain your energy throughout the day:

- Go on a brisk walk (or a fun stroller-ride for them) to get your heart-rate up. Just by exercising, you'll be adding energy into your day, along with increased endorphins which will improve your mood.

- Watch the clock and eat a high-protein energy snack every two to three hours. Fueling your body physically will help you mentally and emotionally, as well.

- Take a "power nap" when the kids go down for their naps. A lack of sleep could be making you feel listless and lifeless. Or, just lie there and relax . . . talk to God or play some worship music and let it soothe your soul.

- Get outdoors. Just feeling the grass under your feet, the sun on your back, or a cool breeze on your face will remind you, again, that life is short and you were created to love God and enjoy Him (and what He's created) forever.

- Find the view—even if it's a butterfly seen from your kitchen window, or a bird perched on your backyard fence. When we see and experience life and beauty, it will focus our minds and freshen our souls.

It feels like just moments ago when I was wishing my daughter was a little older and I could have a little more time to myself. But today, as I finish writing this blog, she is away at college and I am counting the hours until I will see her again.

Remember, dear mom . . . life is short, children grow quickly, and messy houses (and piles of laundry) can wait. So get out of bed, and live this day to the fullest, treasuring the time you have with your little ones while they're still little. You'll never get this day to do over again.

Prayer

Lord, help me live in a way that counts. Give me discernment to know what will last and what will not so I can live wisely. In Jesus' Name, Amen.

SIXTY

We Don't Know What to Do

Shelley Hendrix

We do not know what to do, but our eyes are on You.

2 Chronicles 20:12b (NIV)

One Sunday in June of 2013, my daughter was in a minor fender-bender. Her story was that the guy in the car in front of her backed up and into her on purpose before she could even put her car into reverse to avoid being hit. He said she hit him. He was angry and yelling at her as he got out of his car. He called an ambulance, insisting he was injured by this crash.

I went to the scene to make sure she was okay, and thankfully she was. Her dad had gotten there as well and was helping keep her calm as she was understandably shaken up by all that was happening. I didn't know what to tell her, except this:

"No weapon formed against you will prosper.* Weapons WILL be formed against you, but that doesn't mean they'll win."

I continued to pray that God would show Himself strong on her behalf and increase her faith in His ability to take good care of her. When the policeman arrived, he was trying to make heads or tails of these two conflicting stories. It wasn't too long after that conversation and those prayers that a guy across the street came forward with a video of the WHOLE THING!

The entire scene was captured on tape, showing the car in front of my daughter's BACK UP on purpose to hit her; revealing the driver yelling at her as though she had done something to him. The police officer had a smile on his face as he walked over to the other driver to tell him he was writing up a ticket for HIM.

What a lesson in trusting God when bad stuff happens. It doesn't mean that everything we experience gets tied up with a nice bow on top so quickly, but it does reveal that God is trustworthy, watching out for His own, and that the truth really does eventually come to light.

I am thinking about this as I face an uphill battle of my own: will I choose to trust God in this or will I give in to panic and fret over how I can fix it?

Prayer

Dear Heavenly Father, we don't always know what to do, so in those times, help us to turn our eyes and our attention towards you. Increase our faith as we continue to take steps of obedience even when we don't understand what is happening or why you aren't "fixing" situations for us. In Jesus' Name, Amen.

No weapon formed against you shall prosper . . . Isaiah 54:17a

ABOUT THE EDITOR

Shelley Hendrix is a Wife, Mom, Author, Ministry Leader and Life Coach. She has authored three books, including *On Purpose for a Purpose*, and *Why Can't We Just Get Along?* which was featured in CALLED Magazine's Summer 2013 edition as a "Must Read!" She is also the founder of Church 4 Chicks, 2014 Kingdom Awards' Ministry of the Year honoree, and co-founder of Heart Smart — Counseling, Coaching and Consulting, with her husband and BFF, Stephen.

Shelley's speaking topics include:
- On Purpose for a Purpose
- Dealing with Difficult People
- Finding Peace (even) in Difficult Relationships
- Living an Honest, Authentic, and Real Life
- Learning to Live with Purpose... *Without all the Pressure*
- Relational Peace, Emotional Health, and Spiritual Maturity

Find more about Shelley and her work at www.shelleyhendrix.com and www.church4chicks.com

ABOUT THE CONTRIBUTORS

Anita Agers-Brooks is a Business and Inspirational Coach, international speaker, author, and host of the podcast "Fresh Faith Inspirations with Anita Brooks." She is passionate about business with integrity, healthy relationships, and issues of identity. Anita loves lounging by a lake with her husband, and believes it's never too late for a fresh start with fresh faith. More of Anita Agers-Brooks: www.anitabrooks.com

Jennie Atkins is a manager of two teams of software engineers, one located stateside the other in Mumbai, India. When not at her day job, she writes about individuals who discover God's healing grace while struggling to overcome the mistakes of their past. A native Ohioan, Jennie and her husband of forty years packed up their home and moved to a small valley east of Carson City, Nevada. They have four children and three grandchildren. More of Jennie Atkins: jenniekatkins.blogspot.com

Christina Caro is a pseudo-Yankee, city-loving mother to two spirited little girls, Mirabella and Emerie, and a daredevil toddler son, Deacon. In 2012, she quit her project management job and she and her husband navigated two interstate relocations over the course of two years. She now lives on the Virginia coast and is still adjusting to being home with the kids. She is learning more about giving and accepting grace now than in any other season yet and writes about it all on her blog, www.smarterardor.com.

Deb DeArmond Deb is an author, a speaker, and relationship coach—helping others improve their interactions at work and at home. She is the author of *Related by Chance, Family by Choice: Transforming Mother-in-Law and Daughter-in-Law Relationships* and *I Choose You Today: 31 Choices to Make Love Last.* Her newest book, *Don't Go To Bed Angry. Stay Up and Fight.*, will release in June of 2016. Deb has been married to her high school sweetheart for 42 years lives in the Dallas/Forth Worth area. Find more of Deb DeArmond at debdearmond.com.

Varina Denman is a native Texan who spent her high school years in a rural town. Writing the Mended Hearts series has allowed her to reminisce about small town memories. She and her husband live near Fort Worth, where they enjoy spending time with their five mostly-grown children. Find more of Varina at www.varinadenman.com.

Sue Detweiler is a mother of 6, an author, speaker, and radio host with over 25 years of experience in leadership, ministry and education. When her book, *9 Traits of a Life-Giving Mom*, was launched it hit #1 on Amazon's Hot New Releases for Christian Women's Issues. You can find more of Sue at www.suedetweiler.com.

Jan Dunlap has 33 years of experience raising her five children. She is the author of the humorous memoir *Saved by Gracie*, and the laugh-out-loud Birder Murder Mystery series. Jan lives in Minnesota, where she delights in finding God and laughter in the everyday moments of life to share with her readers and audiences. You can find more of Jan at www.jandunlap.com.

Dena Dyer is a mom, wife, speaker, author and frequent media guest who loves dark chocolate, movies, and all things literary. She serves as a contributing editor for The High Calling (www.thehigh-calling.org) and enjoys spending time with her family, friends, and church (where her husband serves as music/worship minister). More of Dena Dyer: www.denadyer.com.

Kristan Dooley has worked in ministry for over a decade. Equipped with a master's degree in educational ministry from Cincinnati Christian Seminary, Kristan is passionate about taking people to a deeper place in their relationship with Christ. Kristan is the author of *Bigger: Rebuilding the Broken*. She and her husband Dave have two daughters, Ella and Addilyn. Find more of Kristan Dooley at www.kristandooleyblog.com.

Alison Everill is a pastor's wife and the joyful mom of 3 boys. She is also a worship leader, songwriter, vocalist, and speaker who loves to serve the body of Christ by ministering in churches and at ladies events. Her heart's desire is to encourage women to embrace lives of worship. More of Alison Everill: www.alisoneverill.com.

Cheri Fuller is a gifted speaker and award-winning author of over 45 books—including her newest, *Dangerous Prayer: Discovering Your Amazing Story in the Eternal Story of God*. Having been awarded the

Gold Medallion for her coauthored book and twice the Silver Medallion, Cheri's works have sold well over one million copies and impacted people both in the U.S. and around the world. More of Cheri Fuller: www.cherifuller.com.

Katie Gibson is a wife and stay-at-home mom of three, a blogger and the founder of RootedMoms.com. Her desire is to present the truth of God's Word in practical and applicable ways so that others will be encouraged and grow in their relationship with Christ. Follow her and find out more about Rooted Moms at www.rootedmoms.com.

Monica Gill is a devoted Christian wife, mother, and high school history teacher, as well as the founder of Life With Grace. She is a speaker for women's events and retreats and is an active Bible teacher and discipler. Monica has been involved in women's ministry and youth ministry for over twenty years. She would sum up her calling from the Lord as the mission to communicate this one truth: Jesus is the Answer . . . Jesus is always the answer! You can find Monica at www.lifewithgrace.net.

Heather James is the author of *Unholy Hunger* and *Hands of Darkness*. Heather is also a practicing attorney and a newspaper columnist. She lives in California with her husband and two children.

Dorothy Johnson writes from her home on a ridge overlooking the Arkansas River in Little Rock. She has been involved in women's ministries for nearly forty years, teaching Bible studies. Her passion is for people, especially women, to understand their value in Jesus. More of Dorothy Johnson: www.reflectionsfromdorothy.blogspot.com.

Karen Jordan is an author, speaker, writing instructor, and blogger who encourages others to tell the stories that matter most. A native Texan, she and her husband Dan reside in Arkansas, near their two married children and seven grandchildren. Her first book—*Words That Change Everything* (working title)—is scheduled for release in Spring 2016. More of Karen Jordan: www.karenbarnesjordan.com.

Lori Kennedy is the founder of Alpha Omega Ministries. A Christian vocalist and singer, Lori reaches out to others through her inspirational songs and speaking engagements. Her song "Healing Tears" from her most recently released project was nominated one of the top ten songs of 2013 by CWIMA (Christian Women in Media Association). Lori is actively involved as a worship leader and singer for church events and Christian retreats across the United States. To connect with Lori, visit her at www.lorikennedy.com.

Michelle LaRowe is a wife, mother, and the author of *Nanny to the Rescue!, Nanny to the Rescue Again!, Working Mom's 411* and *A Mom's Ultimate Book of Lists*. She is an award-winning nanny and currently serves as the editor-in-chief of eNannySource.com and as executive director of Morningside Nannies. More of Michelle LaRowe: www.michellelarowe.com.

Cheryl Lutz is a lay counselor, writer, and speaker. She is passionate to help others tear down strongholds and find deliverance through Christ. You may connect with and contact her at www.securelyheld.com

Gillian Marchenko is an author and national speaker who lives in Chicago with her husband Sergei and four daughters. She is currently writing a memoir about depression that will publish with InterVarsity Press. She also writes and speaks about stumbling faith, special needs, imperfect motherhood, and deep belly laughs. Find more of Gillian Marchenko at www.gillianmarchenko.com.

Cindi McMenamin is a national speaker and author of several books including *When Women Walk Alone, God's Whispers to a Woman's Heart* and her most recent, *When God Sees Your Tears*. For more on her Southern California-based ministry, see her website, www.StrengthForTheSoul.com.

Jill McSheehy is wife to Matt and mom to Drew and Alyssa. A former manager at a Ford dealership, Jill now stays home with her children. In her spare time she pursues her lifelong dream of writing and teaching. Jill teaches a weekly moms group and serves as Sunday School Director at her church. Follow Jill at www.journeywithjill.net.

Christie Purifoy lives in southeastern Pennsylvania with her husband and four young children. After earning a PhD in English literature, she traded the university classroom for an old farmhouse and a writing desk. You can find more of her writing at www.christiepurifoy.com.

Sherri Sand is an author and speaker. Her unique perspective unlocks truths and biblical mysteries to bring hope to the hurting and peace to the stressed. She desires to lead people into a deeper relationship with God, where living as victorious overcomers becomes the norm rather than an elusive desire. To read her blog and discover more about living in spiritual wholeness and about Sherri's novel, *Leave it to Chance,* visit her web site at www.sherrisand.com.

Stephanie Shott is founder of The M.O.M. Initiative, a ministry that helps churches impact their communities and this culture for Christ through the power of mentoring moms. She is an author and a popular speaker who is called upon by media outlets to share her story of abuse, brokenness, and redemption. More of Stephanie Shott: www.themominitiative.com.

Jennifer Strickland is a dedicated wife, mother of three, inspirational speaker, and author of *More Beautiful Than You Know.* As a former professional model, she once appeared in *Vogue* and *Glamour* and walked the runways of Europe, but since leaving the modeling industry she has founded U R More, a ministry changing the world one heart at a time through events and experiences that reconnect people with the heart of God. For a window into her heart, check out Jen's Journal at www.jenniferstrickland.net

Shellie Rushing Tomlinson is a Jesus-loving, humor-gathering author, speaker, and radio host known as The Belle of All Things Southern. Shellie believes "the whole world stops for a story." She lives in Louisiana and stacks her stories up at www.allthingssouthern.com.

Jennifer Vander Klipp likes making order from chaos—something she gets to do a lot as a mom to two and stepmom to four. A California native transplanted to the Midwest, her favorite thing is discovering with her husband how much there is to love about seasons, snow, and the delight that is Michigan. Jennifer owns a publishing services company helping writers navigate the world of publishing, indie or traditional. She also brings her project management skills to companies who need extra help in the short or long term on creative or communications projects. Find her at www.TandemServicesJVK.com.

Lisa Velthouse is a freelance writer and speaker. Her latest books are *Craving Grace* (a memoir) and Lauren Scruggs' *Your Beautiful Heart* (for teens.) In her work, Lisa strives to explore and share the reality of that grace. Find Lisa's reflections on faith, family, and military life, plus information about her speaking and books, at www.LisaVelthouse.com.

Linda Vujnov is a speaker, writer, blogger, and jogger. She lives in Orange County, California with her husband of 25 years and their 4 kids ranging in age from 12 to 21. She works full time as the Children's Ministry Director at Saddleback Church, Irvine South. To read more devotionals by Linda please visit her blog at lindavujnov.blogspot.com.

Jennifer O. White is the author of *Prayers for New Brides: Putting on God's Armor After the Wedding Dress* and *Marriage Armor for the #PrayingBride.* You can find her offering hope and prayer inspiration based on God's Word at jenniferowhite.com.

Tricia Lott Williford is a widowed single mom raising two young men who could charm you to the moon with their freckles. She collects words, books and bracelets, and she believes the best part of coffee is the feel of the mug in her hand. She is the author of *And Life Comes Back* and *Let's Pretend We're Normal: Adventures in Rediscovering How To Be A Family*. Find her at www.tricialottwilliford.com.

Jessica Wolstenholm is co-founder of Grace for Moms. After 15 years in the music and publishing industries, Jessica came home to be with her two small children. Although the transition from the corporate world to the playground has been an adjustment, she is learning every day to access the grace available to us through Christ as she navigates the full time job of motherhood. She is the co-author of *The Pregnancy Companion: A Faith-Filled Guide for Your Journey to Motherhood* and *The Baby Companion: A Faith-Filled Guide for Your Journey Through Baby's First Year*. Jessica lives in Nolensville, TN with her husband, Dave and two miracle babies, Hope and Joshua. More of Jessica Wolstenholm: www.graceformoms.com

ABOUT THE PUBLISHER

FH Publishers is a division of FaithHappenings.com

FaithHappenings.com is the premier, first-of-its kind, online Christian resource that contains an array of valuable local and national faith-based information all in one place. Our mission is "to inform, enrich, inspire and mobilize Christians and churches while enhancing the unity of the local Christian community so they can better serve the needs of the people around them." FaithHappenings.com will be the primary i-Phone, Droid App/Site and website that people with a traditional Trinitarian theology will turn to for national and local information to impact virtually every area of life.

The vision of FaithHappenings.com is to build the vibrancy of the local church with a true "one-stop-resource" of information and events that will enrich the soul, marriage, family, and church life for people of faith. We want people to be touched by God's Kingdom, so they can touch others FOR the Kingdom.

To learn more, visit www.faithhappenings.com.

www.ingramcontent.com/pod-product-compliance
Lightning Source LLC
LaVergne TN
LVHW011155080426
835508LV00007B/412